C5   op   6 50

handling
the
racing
dinghy

handling
the
racing
dinghy

UWE MARES
and
KURT SCHUBERT

Henry Regnery Company • Chicago

Contents

Preface

No matter where we go, we find we are struck by how often people make mistakes when they are out sailing, not only when cruising, but also when they are racing. What is more we feel sure that these sailors have a good sound basic knowledge—in theory! But even the best of theoreticians is ineffective until he has learnt how to put theory into practice, and this is particularly the case with sailing. Our intention, therefore, has been to show as clearly and graphically as possible the correct way to sail in practice, but at the same time we have not neglected the theoretical background.

With this in mind it was important to express ideas in a clear simple framework, so that they could be easily understood, and this led us to adopt a method whereby tuning and sailing technique are taken as one central theme. In a book which is strongly biased towards sailing in practice, it is in any case not easy to separate these two factors which are always interdependent on the water.

The subject of this book is clearly defined: it concerns the correct handling of modern light displacement dinghies, whether cruising dinghies or racing dinghies, and we have assumed that the reader already has a basic knowledge of sailing. It is not a book for beginners. The twin themes of dinghy tuning and sailing technique on which we concentrate are treated as exhaustively as possible, based on up-to-date knowledge and experience, but without lapsing into the pseudo-knowledgeable realms of speculation.

Inevitably this book has more to offer the racing man than the cruising sailor, even though racing is specifically dealt with in only one chapter. If owners of cruising dinghies feel themselves a bit neglected, we suggest that they should consider the point that, really, getting a boat to sail faster is largely a matter of equipment. Nothing can be done to alter the basic shape of the hull, and from many points of view a cruising dinghy is not very different from a racing dinghy. Any design of boat can achieve a certain maximum speed, and the more discriminatingly and painstakingly she is fitted out, the nearer she will approach that maximum designed speed. The basic principles of tuning a boat, and to a great extent those of sailing technique too, are the same for all dinghies. The fact that the owner of a racing dinghy can get more out of this book than a purely cruising man is only because his boat is better equipped, and he therefore has more opportunity to get the best out of her.

The object of this book, therefore, is to set out as thoroughly and as simply as possible the advanced techniques of dinghy sailing for all helmsmen and crew, and here again is common ground where cruising and racing interests meet, for perfect handling of a dinghy, and the extraction of the last ounce of potential speed, are the aims and wishes of every keen sailor.

Uwe Mares/Kurt Schubert

7

Which is the right boat for you?

At a rough guess something like a quarter or a third of all boat-buyers regret their choice sooner or later, and usually sooner. The reason is very often that the decision to buy a boat is made under pressure, due either to haste or to limitation of cash. Sometimes a purchase is the result of a spontaneous impulse, made without enough thought. Often, and especially when buying secondhand boats, people are all too ready to make a compromise. The result is that neither purely personal considerations nor those outside considerations which influence the choice of type of boat are given enough thought, and light only dawns after the boat has been purchased. It is hardly surprising really, for the variety of types on offer are less easy to inspect than, for example, those on the automobile market; nor is much done to make choice simpler. Enthusiasm for a newly acquired boat wanes rapidly when it becomes clear that another dinghy is far more suitable and performs better. Especially when buying a first boat, lack of experience as to how she will perform brings problems, and vague theories about what is needed only crystallize when the disadvantages of that first purchase become apparent. So, before buying, there are some points worthy of serious consideration.

Personal Inclination

Firstly, the basic aim—what sort of sailing are you interested in? Are you after exciting high-performance sailing, or are you looking for peace and relaxation on the water? As a rule a young family man with wife and child will rarely be able to set his sights on owning a sensitive racing dinghy, while a young energetic hothead is hardly likely to enthuse about a chubby family dinghy. The man with a family who nevertheless wants exciting sailing, should not go for either of these two extremes, for there are many really lively boats which also, to a great extent, satisfy the prime requirements of a family boat, safety and comfort.

Thus dinghies can be divided into three categories:
(a) pure high-performance racing machines
(b) exciting, but nevertheless safe cruising dinghies
(c) safe, comfortable family dinghies.

If high performance is the main consideration, then it must be a fast racing dinghy, and the choice must depend to some extent on the owner's age and physical condition. The question of the crew must also be taken into account, for in a racing dinghy he is much more than simply a sailing companion, and for that reason is also harder to find. When in doubt a single-handed dinghy should also be considered, perhaps the Finn or the equally widely distributed International OK dinghy.

In this group, naturally, are to be found most of the racing fanatics, and they should be quite clear on one point before they buy: the more the class is widely distributed and internationally recognised, the more expensive the boat usually is. A good example is the Olympic Flying Dutchman,

11

the price of which has long been out of proportion to what it offers—at least if it is to be kept in racing trim. There are quite a number of relatively cheap racing dinghies which give just as good scope for racing. It is essential first to find out which classes are sailed most generally in the area.

The man who has no wish to race, and is sure that he never will, does not need to opt for one of the established classes, although they are likely to be the better bet on account of their wide distribution. This is particularly the case with regard to detail improvements, for classes are constantly being modified. There are, however, many well-designed boats which belong to no class, and they usually have the advantage of being cheaper. Boats or classes which are not widely distributed should be really thoroughly looked at.

The man who wants exciting sailing, but who is not keen on too much in the way of acrobatics, will do well to choose a fast cruising dinghy, especially if his wife and children often sail with him, for then safety becomes of greater importance. Such dinghies, of which the Enterprise is a typical example, combine fast sailing with safety and are often ideal for inland waters because they sail well even in light airs, but are relatively safe. The main

The Flying Dutchman has been an Olympic Class since 1960 and today is one of the most refined and fastest racing dinghies in the world. It was designed in 1952 by the Dutch- *man, van Essen, with a length of 6·05 metres, a beam of 1·80 metres, a sail area of 15 sq. metres and a weight of 160 kgs. Almost all the leading Flying Dutchmen are made of plywood.*

points to look for here are stability due to broad flat quarters, which could possibly be hard chine like the G.P.14, good buoyancy forward and at the sides, and a relatively large sail area to give speed. Often these boats have neither spinnaker nor trapeze.

Then there are those boat-buyers whose first aim is comfort, while speed is of only secondary consideration. Particularly suitable for them are real cruising dinghies, perhaps with a spray-hood or a small cabin and a ballast centre-plate. These boats are often less sluggish than they appear, and the best of them are often not much slower than dinghies designed for speed.

Not only is there great demand for boats of this type, but there is also a great danger of making a bad buy, for among the innumerable types on offer quality quite often falls by the wayside, and there are few recognised classes. It is advisable to have an expert inspect the boat and her equipment.

Often people do not have first-hand experience of a boat, and it is difficult to assess one without sailing in her. It is best, therefore, to make enquiries from a number of disinterested people who either own a similar boat, or have some experience of her performance. It may well be that the boat has been tested and re-

Here we can see a typical cockpit and deck layout on one of the latest designs. Note the absence of cross-thwart, but a central mainsheet traveller instead, no after deck, rounded deck edges and light efficient gear. Everything here is geared to high performance sailing using the trapeze.

Because of the increasing shortage of jib hands, single handed dinghies are becoming ever more popular. On the right are Finns—an Olympic class since 1952. Left is a Moth and these two, together with the hard chine OK dinghy, are the most popular single-handers.

ported on in one of the yachting magazines, and this is without doubt the best way of getting a clear picture. Add to this the result of your own deliberations as to what you personally want, and you should make the right choice. Advertising pamphlets not only seem to be unreliable, they often are. Naturally they extol the good points of a boat, but sometimes they also claim characteristics which a boat simply cannot possess by virtue of her very design.

Finally there is a category of dinghy which differs only in size from the racing dinghies already mentioned—boats for young people. The only one which is of basically different construction is the Optimist, aimed at the very youngest. This is an ideal dinghy for children up to ten years old, and they can learn all the first principles of sailing in this little boat. It has no real rivals yet, and has therefore

Even this can be still called a dinghy because it is light and has a centreboard and detachable rudder. But it also has a cuddy and an auxiliary outboard motor and is not designed for racing.

spread world-wide. A child who has grown out of an Optimist usually knows what he wants: the 420, the Vaurien or the Flipper Scow. Of these the 420 has the advantage of being built along the lines of modern racing dinghies, with a spinnaker and, if required, a trapeze.

For the over 16's who have grown out of their boats, the way ahead is clear: if they are going to take up racing seriously the French designed 470, the Fireball or the German Korsar can be considered, but since they are all well equipped, they are priced almost as highly as the ultra specialist racing dinghies. Nevertheless the fact is that they are all, in their re-

This family dinghy has a collapsible spray hood, and is of a stable shape with plenty of reserve buoyancy. (Top.)

This boat looks like a racing dinghy but is not. It is long and lean but heavy and has a fixed keel. It is a fairly typical lake racing boat which would remain afloat on a mooring.

15

The Optimist is the most widely distributed boat for young children and is found all over the world. There is no more suitable dinghy for the younger generation. The box-like hull makes her relatively stable.

This boat has been specially designed for children from 11–about 16 years old who have grown out of Optimists.

spective areas, the most widely distributed classes. We are now talking only of racing dinghies, which come into group (a).

Other considerations

Once personal inclination has been established it is as well to assemble all the other considerations such as conditions in the area where the boat will be sailed, launching and trailing problems, boat park, winter storage and, not least, the inevitable running costs which will arise. So far as the area is concerned, on small inland waters for example, where there are mainly light winds, the safety factor will not be so important as on open coasts. A versatile cruising dinghy which is not stable enough to use as a family boat on the coast could be just right for quiet inland waters. Information about wind and weather conditions is always useful. If the intention is to join a sailing club, it is best to find out which are the adopted classes, for it can be a condition of joining a club that you own a boat belonging to one of the classes sailed there. If the boat is to be stored on land it is as well not to choose too heavy a dinghy, for helping hands or a convenient slip are not always at your disposal. A mooring, which can be cheaper, should only be used if the boat is made of fibreglass, because owing to water soakage plywood boats should not spend a whole season afloat. The man who is sure that he will mostly transport his boat by car will soon succumb to the lure of a so-called car-top dinghy. However, many dinghies which are so des-

cribed are not really suitable for car-top transport, and the weight limit is about 60 to 70 kilogrammes. Very few cruising or racing dinghies can be transported on a car roof, despite the fact that this is steadfastly ignored in advertising pamphlets.

Two popular European designed classes. These boats have all the attributes of modern high performance dinghies, with equipment to match. Top is the West German Korsar. Below the 470, like her French designed sister the 420 and the British designed 505, is already widely distributed and has been allocated as an Olympic class.

Dinghy Hulls and Fittings

Hull Materials

Today, dinghy hulls are almost exclusively made of plastic, that is G.R.P. or A.B.S., or of plywood. GRP is the abbreviation for glass reinforced plastic, while ABS is a purely chemical term—Acrylnitryl-butadienstyrol. Solid wooden hulls must be considered out of date, but there are still some people who are enthusiastic about them in spite of their disadvantages. Even the era of moulded ply is fading. Two of the Olympic Classes, however, the Flying Dutchman and the Finn, were designed specifically for moulded ply construction and are not very suited to synthetic materials, particularly the Flying Dutchman, and they are therefore mostly still built of moulded ply.

The practical advantages of plastic hulls are undeniable, particularly on the grounds of economy. They are not only cheaper, but they are tougher and easier to maintain. The most common method of construction is GRP where glass mat, glass weave and polyester resin are laid up by hand. A few years ago a new thermoplastic material was developed which is abbreviated to ABS. ABS boats are mass-produced and, as has been proved by experience, have the advantage over GRP in that there is no variation in quality.

The keen racing man who has chosen to buy a widely distributed class dinghy should stipulate when ordering the boat from a yard that she should be built to the minimum weight permitted by the class rules, and that includes all fixed fittings. A plywood dinghy in particular will become heavier in the course of time, never lighter, and every kilo too much is dead weight which cannot be used to trim the boat because it is immovable.

Hull and Cockpit Construction

It is not easy to establish how well or badly a plastic dinghy has been built, but there are certain pointers which give a good indication as to quality. First there is the strength of the hull and deck. Dinghies with broad flat bottoms frequently have softer spots there which will flex in a seaway. The result is that not only is speed reduced, but the laminates become fatigued and can break down in these areas. To check this, while the boat is lying at an angle or on her side, press with the heel of the hand at the point where the hull has least stiffening inside. Even the softest spots should give only minimally, at least on the bottom.

Another point to check is safety, by which is meant primarily buoyancy. The fore part of the boat is usually separated from the cockpit by a bulkhead, but check whether the inspection cover is attached inside with a rubber strop which presses it firmly against the seal. Sponge rubber has proved to be the most efficient material for sealing. The same holds good for the many dinghies with inspection covers in side buoyancy tanks, although more dinghies now are being designed in double-skinned form with double-bottoms.

In the case of a long capsize or a leak these buoyancy compartments can fill with water, and for this reason all dinghies should have fixed buoyancy which is usually polystyrene blocks. These are best stowed in the side and forward buoyancy compartments and not in the double-bottoms, so that when the boat is full of water she will float in a relatively stable position, and not tend to capsize again as would be the case if the fixed buoyancy was mainly amidships in the double-bottom. Minimum buoyancy for open dinghies is 120–200 litres, while larger boats, especially those designed as family dinghies, should carry correspondingly more.

Dinghies which are not built in double-skinned form can be checked at two more critical points, namely where the centre-board case and side tanks meet the cockpit floor. Cracks can occur at these joints after they have been subjected to stress. The strength of the centreboard case is often a tricky point, particularly in very lightly built racing dinghies. It must be strong and rigid, and the sides must never distort. When necessary it should be stiffened at the sides and aft with struts so that it cannot possibly distort, for in a seaway it is subject to heavy stresses. The centreboard must be able to move freely up and down in the case, but have no side play for that too reduces speed.

This is a typical racing dinghy layout. The shape of the hull and the comprehensive fittings are primarily designed for speed. A thwart has been included to give the centreboard the necessary strength, and this also serves as a seat when needed.

20

A dinghy with insufficient emergency buoyancy can fill and settle below the water after a lengthy capsize or springing a leak. This not only makes further sailing impossible and makes it more difficult to lower the sails, but can endanger life.

This picture shows a simply equipped small all-purpose dinghy for an equally small family. Generous seating makes her comfortable, and the high-sided hull is designed for stability. A closed locker has been built into the stern thwart. Compare with the photo opposite.

21

There are optimum proportions of length, depth and thickness of rudder and centreboard. This is interesting in that the Olympic dinghy classes, and many other internationally distributed classes as well, are only permitted to use rudders and centreboards of quite different proportions. The rudder illustrated below is well shaped, both as seen from the side and also from below.

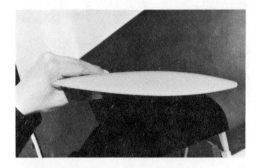

The Cockpit and Fittings

How much thought has gone into the design of a boat can readily be seen in the layout of the cockpit, both in the shape of the deck and the inside of the cockpit, and also in the arrangement and efficiency of the fittings. Naturally a racing dinghy will be equipped with much more comprehensive and specialised fittings, while a good well-designed family dinghy will have comfortable broad thwarts and a high solid coaming which can be used both as a back rest and to provide some shelter from wind and spray. Sailing qualities should not have been neglected, but it is inevitable that small concessions to comfort will also detract slightly from performance.

A great number of the details that should be checked are common to all types of dinghy. Beginning at the stern, first check the rudder. The essentials are an uphaul and a downhaul for the rudder blade if of the lifting type, and a safety catch to prevent the whole rudder assembly from detaching itself during a capsize when it could drift away or sink. In higher performance boats it is as important to have a tiller extension with a convenient catch to hold it fast when folded in as to have side tanks nicely rounded off to make sitting out more comfortable. Toe-straps on such boats should be divided and separately adjustable for helmsman and crew.

Watch out that the main sheet arrangement is efficient and can be properly cleated, for otherwise heavy weather will

22

not be much fun. Musts are a non-slip cockpit floor, and a roughened side deck where the trapeze hand stands. The kicking-strap must be effective and easy to adjust, there should be a good cleating system for the jib, and the jib fairlead itself should be mounted so that its position can be altered as much as is needed. All these points are just as important in a cruising dinghy as in a racing dinghy. Supposing on the other hand that you find badly fastened fittings with sharp edges, protruding screws or stressed fixtures with insufficient backing. Then you have every reason to doubt the quality of a boat, and you can be pretty sure that other tests will prove equally unsatisfactory.

Comfortably rounded sides for sitting out are extremely important for racing dinghies. The boat must have accurately adjustable toe-straps so that a sitting out position is possible which is comparatively effortless, and which can therefore be maintained for long periods. A good mainsheet system like this one means that sailing in strong winds is not torture but a real pleasure.

23

The Rig and the Sails

THE MAST, STANDING AND RUNNING RIGGING

Mast—Materials and Shapes

If you compare the hull of a boat to the body of a motorcar, then the rig can be likened to the engine. Propulsion is provided by the sails and indirectly by the mast, boom, standing and running rigging. While nothing can be done to change the shape of a boat's hull, the speed of a boat is influenced by the tuning of the rig, and it can be influenced both for better and for worse. It is no wonder that intensive experiment and development has taken place in this field for years. The fact that a Flying Dutchman today is half as fast again as when the class was first introduced is almost entirely due to new knowledge about the workings of masts and sails.

Wooden masts nowadays are a thing of the past. Not only the racing sector, but cruising sailors too, predominantly use metal masts and booms. Even the cheapest boats use aluminium spars, and alterations to class rules have for some years allowed the use of aluminium masts in the most traditional of all, the Olympic classes.

The main advantage of metal masts over wooden is the same as that of plastic boats over wooden ones—greater durability. There is also the reduction in maintenance costs, for aluminium tubing is anodised which prevents oxidisation in salt water. The warping which occurs in wooden masts due to weather or bad storage cannot happen.

This does not mean that all metal masts are of equal quality for, quite apart from the question of the right section, they must be made of a pure alloy of sufficient strength. The metal must be properly annealed because otherwise, if the mast is bent for any reason, it will not be able to regain its former shape.

The production and care of an aluminium mast presents no problems. If the mast is straight, properly annealed and well anodised its life is unlimited, and this is in direct contrast to a wooden mast which generally starts to show signs of fatigue after two or three years, after which it will get weaker and weaker until, one day, it breaks in a gust. At present aluminium is the best material for masts, and in spite of the fact that there are a great number of experiments going on with other materials and construction methods, up to now they have not resulted in any improvements so far as mass production is concerned.

A good aluminium mast must always be a successful compromise between minimum weight, minimum wind resistance, low centre of gravity and sufficient strength and moments of inertia. There is a great variety of different sections, each with its advantages and disadvantages. The most popular is almost pear-shaped, with the metal carefully distributed to give the greatest strength so that the mast can be built with thinner walls and so save weight. The section of a mast does not remain constant from truck to heel, but tapers conically above the forestay. This allows the top of the mast to bend both aft and to either side as is

(Photograph on page 25)
Mast and sail nowadays are looked on as an indivisible unit. Interdependence is so great that even the most successful boats often race an entire season or more with one suit of

sails if these match well with the mast. A good all-round sail can nowadays be adjusted to suit all weathers when set on a matching mast.

necessary in strong winds. So far as the stiffness of the mast is concerned, the basic rule is: a soft mast for a light crew—a rigid mast for a heavy crew.

Many metal masts nowadays are filled with polystyrene. Some have pea-like grains poured into them, some have shaped polystyrene blocks forced into them, and some are completely foam-filled. This does not prevent a capsized boat from turning upside down as is commonly thought, but it can help considerably when righting a dinghy because little or no water can get inside the mast, and the crew therefore have less weight to raise when righting the boat.

Methods of Staying a Mast

Only a short while ago a cult evolved which led to the very exact control of bending a mast in any part of its length by means of stays. Consequently masts were very thin and light. This fashion is already on the wane, because it was soon found that all the additional struts and wires (standing rigging) resulted in so many small eddies that the airflow to the mainsail was too much affected. A lighter mast and reduced wind resistance could not compensate for the disadvantages of increased turbulence. Nowadays the tendency is to have spreaders which can be adjusted in length to alter the tension or compression of the main stays. They can also be adjusted as to their horizontal angle with the mast. Spreaders govern the amount of bend between the foot of the mast and the hounds (where the stays

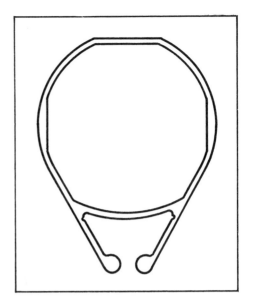

join the mast).

There are fully swinging spreaders which can swing from forward to aft through an arc of 180°. These spreaders, which should always work in tension, have their disadvantages. For example the mast can suddenly bend aft if the spreaders should come under compression on a hard spinnaker run, which is quite possible because the spinnaker is then pulling the top part of the mast forward while the middle part will tend to bend aft. The effectiveness of fully swinging spreaders, therefore, is in the first place dependent on the tension of the shrouds. In brief: if the length of the spreaders is increased, the mast will bend more: if they are shortened, the mast will be straighter.

Currently most popular are the limited-swing spreaders which allow far better control of mast bend. Again there are two

The section illustrated above has proved to be very efficient for today's aluminium masts. It tapers conically towards the masthead.

variable factors, the adjustable length of the strut and the adjustable angle. The spreaders should be fixed once the correct setting has been found. As a rough guide, when the mast is straight the spreaders should push the stays a few centimetres out of line. As to the angle, the spreaders should be fixed so that the stays are drawn slightly forward of straight. If the mast is to bend slightly further forward but not sideways, the angle of the spreaders should be fixed a little further aft without altering the length. However, to bend the mast to windward and so open the slot between main and jib, leave the angle unchanged but shorten the length of the spreaders. The middle of the mast will then bend away from the fore-and-aft line. As regards height, where masts are stepped through the deck the spreaders should be just above the half way point between the deck and the forestay attachment. Where the mast is stepped on deck they should be just under the half way point.

An alternative, but increasingly less popular method of staying a mast, is by using diamonds. Their range of adjustment is more limited because basically they prevent sideways bend and to a certain extent they limit fore-and-aft bending too, especially if they are angled slightly forward. The tension of diamonds can be adjusted at their lower ends by means of a lever or drum winch. The main disadvantage of diamonds lies in the fact that the mast is then held so rigidly that it cannot cushion the effect of the waves on the hull when sailing to windward.

The limited swing spreaders on this mast are very effective as they can also be adjusted as to length. The diamonds below them which are angled forwards can, as is explained, have disadvantages.

28

The Function of the Stays
(or Shrouds)

If a simple rig is used consisting only of forestay and two shrouds, then care should be taken that the hounds are lower than when spreaders or diamonds are carried: that is, they should be about one-third of the way down from the truck of the mast. Otherwise, even in moderate winds, sideways bend between the hounds and the foot will be excessive. It is only moderately recently that tuning by means of shroud adjustment has been developed. On high performance racing dinghies at least, the good old bottlescrew or lanyard has given way more and more to light tackles, winches or levers which make tensioning shrouds a rapid action. The positioning of the lower ends of the shrouds should not be neglected either. The further aft the shrouds come, the safer will the mast be when the wind is free, but the boom can then not be let out so far, so a compromise has to be found between these conflicting requirements. If the shrouds are led as far forward as possible, they must be strong and attached to a rigid hull. Under no circumstances should the shrouds lead forward of an athwartships line 30 cm aft of the foot of the mast.

On the 505 (above) the shrouds are connected to a boxed wire tackle so that the helmsman can adjust the tension of the shrouds. On the Fireball (below) a simple lever does the job.

The Halyards

It ought to be obvious that the wire part of halyards should be sufficiently long, but this is not always the case, particularly in family dinghies. Where dinghies carry more than 10 square metres of sail (108 sq. ft.) it is essential that there should be enough wire to extend from the head of the sail to the cleat or fitting, with no rope tail intervening. There should also be a proper method of getting the necessary luff tension. Rope halyards stretch quickly which allows the luff to slacken and, especially so far as the jib is concerned, when the luff sags aft and to leeward, causes the shape of the sail to alter.

Too little wire in the halyards or insufficiently tautened halyards cause the luff to sag, especially where the jib is concerned, and this allows the fullness to shift aft and causes the sail to 'close' on the leech.

Standing and Running Rigging materials

Standing and running rigging these days are made of stainless and synthetic materials, even on the cheapest boats. Galvanised wire, which started to rust at the latest after one season's use in salt water, has almost entirely been superseded by stainless steel. Eyes in halyards and shrouds are no longer fashioned with a rope or wire splice, but instead swaged terminals or Talurit splices are used. In swaging, the wire is led through a stainless hollow tube and the whole is pressed together by rollers. Talurit splices consist of a hollow metal tube, either of aluminium or copper, which is pushed over the wire and then squeezed under pressure. The soft metal penetrates into the heart of the wire and holds the strands together. Many a keen racing sailor today now has his own pressure appliance and tubes in his toolbox so that he can effect repairs in a very short time which in earlier days were laborious and time-consuming.

The Boom

Almost as much experiment has gone into booms as into masts. They used to be box-shaped or round, they either bent downwards and sometimes sideways as well, or were absolutely rigid. In the main, nowadays booms are pretty stiff in all directions and, in contrast to masts, it seems that they are likely to remain so.

That aluminium booms are better than wooden ones is as obvious as with masts. They have a track for the foot of the sail, and are hollow so that a line attached to the clew can be led forward inside the boom to appear at a point where the crew can adjust the tension of the foot of the mainsail while sailing.

The best aluminium booms also have a continuous track along the bottom to accommodate movable slides for both mainsheet and kicking-strap. The importance of adjustable mainsheet blocks for sail tuning is undisputed. If the blocks lie close together, the pull is concentrated at one point, whereas if they are separated the pull is distributed equally over a greater area. If the blocks are fixed further aft, pressure is applied to the mast when the boom is close-hauled causing the lower part of the mast to bend forward.

A mainsheet lead from the end of the boom to the transom is not only inconvenient because both sheet and tiller come from aft, but has disadvantages so far as speed is concerned.

The boom will bend just opposite to the ideal, such as upwards in the centre. A centre sheet lead is both more practical and more efficient.

Shape and Theory

The predominance of synthetic materials does not falter when it comes to sails. Today they are almost exclusively made of man-made fibres which, although basically the same, have different names in various countries: in England Terylene, in America Dacron, in Germany Diolen. These sails are long-lived and need very little attention. They are resistant to damage and have the advantage of needing no stretching, but none of this alters the fact that the development of sails is undergoing a revolution, the revolution of shape.

Dr. Manfred Curry's theory, which is that a sail is like a bird's wing, has served out its time. First postulated in 1925, the bird's wing principle was accepted until fairly recently. But even after it had been realised that this was not the most effective shape for a sail, technical advances had been insufficient to put this knowledge to good use. For a long time nothing could be done about that inconvenient characteristic of sails of losing shape in increasing winds, even when the edges were stretched or the mast was bent. Quite simply, the weave was too open.

In accordance with the bird's wing theory, fullness used to be cut in close aft of the luff where it would hold shape best and be most effective. Laterly both theory and practice have proved conclusively that, in order to enable a boat to point as high and sail as fast as possible, the most effective method is to cut a sail with a

The attachment of the mainsail tack to the boom needs a little care. This bolt with a folding end is one of the best arrangements.

The lower picture shows a track riveted to the underside

of the boom between the gooseneck and kicking-strap. Just aft of the kicking-strap is a hole through which the clew outhaul comes. This can be quickly and easily adjusted and cleated while the boat is under way.

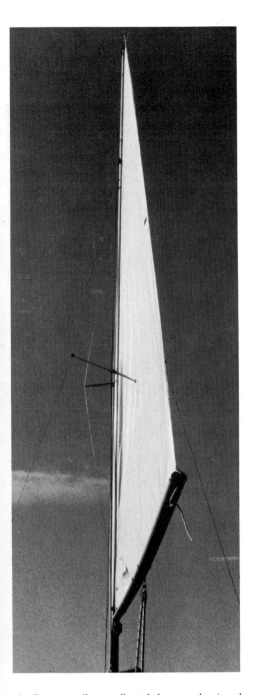

An all-purpose sail on a well matched mast can be trimmed as flat as this in heavy weather . . .

. . . and the same sail set on the same mast is trimmed for light weather. Mast and boom are now almost straight and the edges of the sail are slack.

constant curve and maximum fullness in the centre. All boats, whether old or new, point up to five degrees higher on the wind with a modern sail than they could a short while ago. This became a practical proposition after the successful weaving of a cloth which would keep its shape under heavy wind pressure. Even two or three years ago fullness in the centre of the sail was pushed aft in strong winds, thus adversely affecting speed and pointing.

However, the major problem facing all sailmakers is still to cut a sail the right shape. After selecting suitable cloth, he will cut a trial sail to establish what curves and seams will be needed for a sail which sets well, and above all pulls well. Once he is happy with his trial sail he can make patterns from which further identical sails can be cut, but he must always check that all the cloth is of the original quality and has the right characteristics.

Thus an effective sail will have fullness built into the centre by means of curved cloths sewn together roughly parallel to each other. The position and depth of fullness are decided by the position and amount of the curvature in the cloths. The bolt rope is slightly under tension when it is sewn to the sail, so that when the halyard is slack the cloth is drawn together slightly, making little creases along the edges. Nowadays the luff of the jib has a pocket inside which the luff wire runs.

The tension of the jib must be as quickly and easily adjusted as that of the mainsail. Here the luff downhaul passes through the tube of the furling gear.

The foot of the jib should sweep the deck as in this picture. Any excess of cloth can fold to lie quietly on the deck.

The luff wire is attached to the head of the jib, and this enables the tension of the luff of the jib to be altered under way by pulling down or easing the tack.

Manufacture of Sailcloth

Whether a cloth is good or bad depends on the way in which the polyester threads are woven, and how the woven cloth is treated afterwards. The quality of the polyester threads themselves depends on whether they have been heavily or lightly spun. Those that have been heavily spun crinkle more easily. This is an important point if a very dense cloth is desired, for the threads will then lie close above and below each other. A heavily twisted thread will also stretch more easily under load, as the fibres have room to press more closely together and the thread therefore becomes thinner and longer. The result is

It is not a good idea to have the foot cut too high as in this picture because the wind can then flow from the high pressure side under the foot to the low pressure side of the sail, tending to equalise pressure and consequently reduce drive.

a cloth which stretches relatively easily in both warp and weft. It is possible to control the strength of the cloth in both directions by varying the density of the weave and the type of polyester thread.

Surface finishing also influences the strength and the smoothness of the cloth. The woven cloth is cleaned and run over hot cylinders. It is then stabilised by the application of resin in which it is soaked before passing through rollers which push the resin into the weave. The effect of the resin is to discourage movement of the individual fibres, which also increases the strength. Variation in the finishing process gives the woven cloth those characteristics required for some particular purpose, whether for use on dinghies or on keel boats, for mainsails or for jibs. Thus the characteristics of a cloth are influenced by the strength of the fibres and thread, by the viscosity of the resin, the tension of the loom and the pressure of heat and resin. For this reason careful sailmakers are more and more taking to testing sailcloth *in the round* so as to establish their individual characteristics and to decide whether they are suitable.

Battens

Battens control the shape of the leech of the mainsail. The uppermost is often full length to prevent a fold forming ahead of it. The shape of the sail towards the leech is controlled by their flexibility, soft battens allowing a considerable degree of curve, stiff battens but little. All battens are tapered so that the forward end is more

The uppermost batten should normally be as flexible as this, very soft forwards and stiffer in the after two-thirds.

flexible than the rest, but the uppermost of course is stronger than the others. In the Olympic classes it is easy to see that battens are becoming much shorter since the quality of sail cloth has been so greatly improved. The shape of a sail can now usually be controlled with shorter battens, and that means that the smooth curve of the mainsail can flow further aft before being broken by relatively hard long battens. Today plastic, wood, or a sandwich of wood and plastic is used. Wood is still popular, and is preferred in Australia, New Zealand and Brazil for there they have stronger and more flexible types of timber. The important thing is that a batten should not warp, should be straight when not under load, and should bend evenly.

36

The Spinnaker

Originally the spinnaker was used purely before the wind with the object of increasing the surface area of the sails. Later it was gradually realised that the basic principles of laminar airflow applied as much to the spinnaker as to the mainsail and jib. Development has been the result of this knowledge. On modern dinghies and keelboats spherically cut spinnakers with curved luffs and horizontal cloths predominate. In contrast to earlier spinnakers with vertical cloths, these horizontal seams run in the same direction as the airflow and therefore offer less resistance. Light nylon material stretches less in the warp than in the weft and, therefore, even in strong winds, fullness will not increase.

Spherically cut spinnakers consist of cloths with not one straight edge, and the degree of curvature here too decides the depth of the fullness. They can be spherical or cut with high shoulders. The idea of giving the sail broad shoulders so as to have maximum cloth up high where the blanketing effect of the mainsail is least and the wind speed is higher, has for a long time now ceased to be the main consideration of progressive sailmakers. The tops of their spinnakers designed for modern planing dinghies like the Flying Dutchman are cut up to 15 cm. narrower than the maximum permitted by the class rules for, they argue, only as flat a spinnaker as possible will give maximum drive. They reject the notion that the higher and broader the shoulders of the spinnaker,

A well-cut spherical spinnaker looks like this. Usually it is designed to be a happy compromise between a sail with maximum reaching and running qualities.

37

the faster will the boat sail, and they believe, like the North Americans, that high shoulders cannot produce maximum drive. A flatter spinnaker has less heeling moment, it sets more steadily and can be used at an angle up to 60° to the apparent wind. Hardly anybody disputes that the greatest advantages of flatter spinnakers show up in stronger winds. For broad reaches and runs, and for light weather, a rounder and fuller cut spinnaker is preferable because it collapses less quickly and draws better, especially in calm waters. So anyone with serious ideas about racing will hardly manage to make do with only one spinnaker.

Whether a spinnaker is well cut or not can rarely be decided at first glance, but only by trying it out. Above all the leeches must not be stitched too tightly, for they will then roll inwards too easily. The opposite, however, can be almost as bad, for then they will be too loose and flap about. It does not matter if the top part of the spinnaker flaps its ears a bit, because that shows that it is being trimmed at the optimum angle, in fact on a reach the luff should flutter a bit where it curves at the top and the spinnaker should be played continuously by the crew.

Obvious though the advantages of this new spinnaker shape may be, other advances are questionable, for example cloth weight. Some sailmakers produce spinnakers which, to take an extreme case, are only half the normal weight at about 20 grams per square metre. The advantages of such a light weather sail are so small that they are overshadowed by the disadvantages, namely the increased sus-

ceptibility to tearing and to damage by weather, and particularly from ultra-violet rays.

Black spinnakers too, which were all the rage a short while ago, have not been successful in practice. Using the principle of a hot air balloon, the black material should have produced a tendency towards rising air, but in practice this did not have the desired effect of helping the spinnaker to stand better in light weather. On the

Different spinnaker shapes can be seen racing. FD 1069 has a high-shouldered spinnaker, while FD 943 has a much rounder one.

All spinnakers are appreciably flatter than a few years ago, and on very close reaches the sheet should be led as far aft as possible to get the greatest drive.

other hand the use of multi-coloured spinnaker cloths is not only decorative. The spinnaker can be more closely observed when the sun is shining brightly, and can therefore be better trimmed.

Naturally, thin spinnaker cloth is more liable to damage than that of other sails. It also has a tendency to shrink in heat and to stretch when wet. It is a false but general belief that the spinnaker does not need to be put away so carefully as the other sails. But he who bundles it up when he stows it away will have a smaller sail next time he hoists it, just as a crumpled up bank note, which is flattened out after a time, is no longer as large as one that has been carefully put away—although unlike a spinnaker it is worth just as much.

The spinnakers on these two boats are different again. The left one is relatively flat and is very narrow in the head, so should be particularly effective when reaching in heavy winds. The spinnaker on the right has the typical 'hen-breasted' cut of earlier sails with a centre seam. It is excellent for running, but there are disadvantages on a reach.

Tuning and Handling a Dinghy

In order to sail a modern dinghy at maximum speed it is essential to understand her equipment and its functions. Maximum speed results only from perfect co-ordination of tuning the rig, balancing the boat and proper weight distribution— plus correct sailing technique. Whereas really polished sailing technique, which is the effective combination of physical effort, steering, trimming sails etc., is a case of personal experience and talent and can only be suggested in the broadest possible terms, the tuning of a boat is quite different.

Here it is not so much experience and talent that make for superiority, but rather an understanding of the theory behind the various aspects of tuning, based on cause and effect. Although the point is soon reached when only the practical application of theory can lead to further advances, it is first essential to have sound knowledge of how the various aspects of tuning affect one another. That holds good as much for family dinghies as for high performance racing dinghies, although naturally to a lesser degree, for the broad principles do not change.

As tuning and handling are difficult to deal with separately, we have decided to cover them both in one chapter which, for the sake of clarity, is broken down into sections covering different courses in relation to the wind, and also into different wind strengths. But first we will look closely at tuning a boat and at using a trapeze.

TUNING A BOAT

Weight Distribution, Balance and Tuning the Rig

As is well known, a boat meets two main forms of resistance when sailing through the water. Firstly there is wave-making resistance, which in this context is of only minor importance because it is decided by the design of the boat. Secondly there is frictional resistance, which arises through the motion of the boat through the water. The greater the wetted surface of the boat, the greater the frictional resistance, and therefore the greater the energy required to move the boat forward.

The most effective means of reducing the wetted surface is by shifting weight. If the crew sit further forward the boat will float deeper forward, but the broad stern will be lifted further out of the water. The displacement of the boat will remain the same, but the centre of buoyancy of the hull is changed. The result is that the wetted surface is reduced, and with it the frictional resistance.

If the crew move their weight further aft, the opposite occurs. By lowering the stern the wetted surface increases and the draught forward is decreased. In light airs when frictional resistance is of major importance, the reduction of the wetted surface by suitable adjustment of weight is of particular benefit. In stronger winds, or at higher speeds when other dynamic forces are at work, frictional resistance takes on a subordinate role.

While on this point it is worth while bearing in mind that frictional resistance can also be reduced by careful preparation of the bottom. Only a few years ago it was thought that a highly polished hull was the right answer, but practice backed by experiments has shown that a slightly roughened surface is best. So the surface of the bottom should be rubbed down microscopically finely with sandpaper, and this assists the formation of a thin layer between the bottom and the laminar flow of water streaming past, so reducing frictional resistance. Experiments have shown that wet-or-dry sandpaper of 400 grade is the best.

Where plastic dinghies are concerned,

rubbing down like this can have unfortunate consequences which do not concern plywood boats. There is a danger of rubbing down the gelcoat, the coloured outer layer of the laminate, too much which reduces the strength and waterproof nature of the surface laminate. There is, however, special graphite paint which can be applied. The disadvantage here is that adhesion is not very good, and before long the paint comes off. Incidentally the word *bottom* is not really right, for the whole of the outside of the hull right up to the gunwale should be dealt with. Only too often is it forgotten that the topsides also, to a certain extent, are pushed through the water, and underwater treatment should therefore always extend as far as the gunwales. Anyone seriously

Reduction of the wetted surface by weight shifting is particularly important in light airs, for then friction amounts to 80–90 per cent of the total resistance. But excessive heeling can adversely effect the drive of the sails, so both factors must be taken into account.

Moving weight forward is the other method of reducing the wetted surface which, in the picture above, is carried to too great an extreme as the crew here is disturbing the airflow over the jib.

If the crew sits in the normal amidships position the transom dips right under water which increases the wetted surface and means increased drag.

attempting to obtain maximum speed from his dinghy should not overlook this detail, but nevertheless correct weight distribution is always far more important than a carefully prepared hull.

In contrast to the keelboat sailor, a dinghy sailor is able to alter the boat's lateral resistance. The lateral area concerned is all that part of the boat which lies below the waterline, and this includes both the centreboard and the rudder. This is the total area which is resistant to sideways drift or leeway. It is possible to alter the distribution of the area of lateral resistance by moving the centreboard and the rudder, and also by changing weight distribution. In some modern dinghies the centreboard can be adjusted as to its angle in the centreboard case, and as well the pivot can be

shifted 10–20 cm. forward or aft.

Balancing a boat consists of balancing the relationship between the centre above the water, that is the Centre of Effort (CE) of the sails, and the centre below the water, i.e. the Centre of Lateral Resistance (CLR). The relationship of these two centres to each other is decided by a number of factors such as the course that a boat is sailing, its speed, angle of heel, and the fullness and trim of both sails, for the CE is that of the mainsail and jib combined, except of course in the case of single-handed dinghies with no jib. If the CE lies close astern of the CLR the boat will tend to luff, that is she will have weather helm. If, on the other hand, the CE of the sails lies well forward of the CLR, then the opposite will occur and

A well-trimmed boat will have almost neutral helm even in strong winds when almost all boats tend towards weather helm. This tendency can be countered by the methods explained in the text. Otherwise weather helm will be so *pronounced that it can only be corrected by permanent and tiring use of the rudder (picture) and that means loss of speed.*

she will have lee helm, and then, if the helm is kept in the neutral midships position, the boat will bear away.

Quite apart from all these points it is essential to decide on a basic position for the heel of the mast and the best angle of rake. This is best found by trial and error, stepping the mast in such a way that the helm is neutral in about Force 2 winds with the dinghy pointing high on the wind, the centreboard lowered, the sail trimmed correctly and the weight concentrated in the middle of the boat with almost no angle of heel. Then in lighter winds she will tend to increase lee helm, and conversely when the wind is stronger to more weather helm, but as these tendencies will occur after the norm has been established they can be corrected relatively easily as explained later. This balancing of the CE and the CLR is essential in all weathers and on all courses if the boat is to sail as fast as possible, for otherwise the rudder will have to be used to oppose a tendency to lee or weather helm, and that effectively puts on the brake.

The most complicated factor of all is the tuning of the rig, for not only is the CE altered when any adjustment is made, but also the rig must be tuned in such a way that the sails will develop maximum drive in any given conditions. This can only happen when the mast matches the sails as perfectly as possible. The two together should form a perfect whole, where every change in the shape of the sail is matched by a corresponding bend in the mast. This interaction is naturally far more important for modern racing dinghies than for family dinghies with less refined equipment. In general though, however well cut a sail may be, its potential will never be fully realised unless the mast matches it.

The Technique of Trapezing

The introduction of the trapeze in the middle of the 1950s added a new dimension to dinghy sailing. The trapeze first developed on account of the designing of ever more sensitive and unstable light displacement dinghies with relatively large sail areas which could not be controlled by traditional sitting out methods. Naturally the art of trapeze sailing has refined in the course of years. At first it was a question of standing out on the wire as long as the ache in one's kidneys allowed, but today the problem is to use the weight of the body as effectively as possible by means of various tricks. Technical problems have mostly been ironed out long ago.

Thus today there are hardly any stiff, hard hip harnesses in use, but instead a sort of trapeze corset. Pressure is no longer concentrated on the small area of the hips, but is spread evenly over the whole body by this trapeze corset in which the jib-hand lies as if in a hammock, in a position that is less tiring than normal sitting out. The position of the hook, which must open downwards so that it can easily be disengaged on capsizing, can be adjusted by straps so that the centre of gravity lies just where it is most effective.

The technique of sitting out a modern racing dinghy has become a case of instinct and feeling, where not only strength and quick reactions are needed from the crew, but rather a feel for the response of the boat. It is this combination of qualities which singles out a good trapeze artist, and it is only with such a crew that spectacular racing success will be achieved. Trapeze sailing demands real crewing, because every movement of the helm requires a corresponding reaction from the crew. Where two people sail together in complete understanding, and the need to give orders has long since become unnecessary, the boat will always be found in the front of the fleet in hard races. For many years now a highly tuned Flying Dutchman has been likened more to a sensitive highly-strung horse than to a lifeless piece of sporting equipment.

Due to today's flexible rig, the weight and height of the crew no longer play anything like the same part as when trapezes were first introduced. It is far more important that the trapeze hand should be fit, for then a third or fourth water-soaked woolly jersey can confidently be added to his chest. Top it with a life jacket and trapeze harness, and he will look more like an American footballer than a tender youth!

Although in really boisterous weather a heavy and proportionately tall jib-hand can be an advantage, when beating anyway, in light or moderate winds up to Force 4 there is much to be said for having a capable but light crew, above all on broad reaches with a spinnaker set. A

This trapeze artist is standing at the ideal angle of 90° to the mast. While he is holding the jib sheet in one hand, the other is free so that he can use it to increase leverage or to pull himself back into the boat with the handle at any time.

sensitive trapeze hand can get a 505, a 470 or a Flying Dutchman planing in Force 3 winds, always providing that he works in close harmony with the helmsman.

Trapeze work on the wind offers the jib hand less opportunity, but it is also nothing like so tiring as a planing reach and is therefore a good time to take a breather. All the same, on a beat good trapeze work can squeeze out those few decisive yards, and basically this is a matter of fitness. A

man who can maintain a fully extended position with hollowed back and his free hand in the nape of his neck during the whole of a beat and then make quick tacks can count himself among the fittest. The moot point as to whether it is better to throw the free arm fully back to gain extra leverage, or whether this is countered by increased wind resistance, can be solved by a minor modification. Instead of throwing the arm out fully, if it is pressed into the nape of the neck it is by

On reaching courses the trapeze hand must move his weight fairly far aft. So as to prevent slipping the gunwale should be well roughened as far back as the helmsman.

Too closed a hook is far more dangerous in a risky situation like this where a capsize is likely, for then the harness cannot be detached quickly enough.

50

no means ineffective, particularly with the additional weight of wet pullovers when it will weigh twice as much as normal, and there is no additional wind resistance.

The difficulties which every beginner faces on first trying trapeze sailing are relatively quickly overcome once the basic ideas have been grasped. There are, of course, slight variations for different types of boat. Some dry land training improves the co-ordination of the various movements.

The easiest method of climbing out in a trapeze in a light displacement dinghy goes like this. Already hooked on to the wire the jib hand sits on the side deck just aft of the shroud, and pulls his forward leg up on to the deck, bracing himself against the shroud attachment with his foot. As the jib sheet will have to be trimmed while he is stretching out, the wire is under slight tension while he is sitting on the deck. Pushing against the shroud with his forward foot, he shoves himself out and aft over the gunwale until the whole weight of his body is taken by the wire. He can still hold on to the strop or handle with his forward hand while his after hand copes with the jib sheet. Simultaneously he draws up the other leg and puts his second foot on the gunwale. When

This trapeze equipment is very good. Although ideally shaped, the hook should be rather closer to the body. The jib hand is lying in the trapeze harness as if in a hammock, and the hook is at the body's centre of gravity where it will be most effective. A tackle between the ring and the toggle allows the trapeze hand to adjust its length while on the wire.

he is right out on the wire, with straight legs slightly straddled, the position of his body should be at an angle of 85–90° to the mast. It is not always easy to maintain this angle as the harness straps tend to give a bit. Resourceful trapeze hands cope with this by rigging a tackle between the hook and the trapeze wire, the end of which can be belayed by jamming it between the cam-like inner walls of the upper block. By tightening or releasing the tackle the crew can quickly, and with minimum effort, alter the angle at which he is lying.

When the wind eases the trapeze hand first crouches, then lets his feet slide over the side deck into the cockpit, and then pulls himself in on to the deck by the handle or strop, holding the jib-sheet in his other hand all the while. The alternative method which is so often practised by beginners is for the jib hand to let his body swing so far aft that he lands on deck, but this is not to be recommended as it hampers the helmsman and, furthermore, puts the weight too far aft which is a disadvantage when beating and affects the trim of the dinghy.

TUNING AND SAILING TECHNIQUE CLOSE-HAULED

How can I make most distance to windward in all weather conditions? This question is answered as comprehensively as possible in the following sections. Both the tuning of the boat and sailing technique are decided primarily by two factors, the strength of the wind and the state of the sea, and the same can be said for every point of sailing. In addition to correct technique, maximum speed results from the combination of two basic ingredients: firstly the trim and balance of the hull, in other words weight distribution and the adjustment of the CLR: secondly tuning the rig, the effective adjustment of mast and sails. Only he who understands how these two interact, and how their relationship one to the other changes constantly, will be able to sail his boat at maximum speed and gain most ground to windward.

This is a typical position just before swinging out on a trapeze. The foresheet hand braces himself against the shroud and gunwale with his forward foot. He then pushes himself out from the boat, and at the same time draws up the other leg. He is holding on with his forward hand to the very necessary handle on the trapeze, and is playing the jib sheet with his other hand.

Beating in Light Airs

This section covers tuning and sailing technique in light winds up to about Force $1\frac{1}{2}$. How to trim the boat in this weather has already been explained. The wetted surface should be reduced as much as possible because at such low speeds surface friction makes up 80–90 per cent of the total resistance. Thus the crew must sit far enough forward to raise the transom completely clear of the water. This is primarily the job of the jib hand because the helmsman has less freedom of movement. In most dinghies the jib hand needs to sit forward of the weather shroud, level with the mast; this is normally at the after end of the foredeck. He can then lean far enough to leeward to make the

The weight of the crew is well placed in the prevailing light airs. However the jib of this 505 should be eased slightly.

dinghy heel slightly, further reducing the wetted surface. While the lee side of the boat dips deeper into the water, the actual area is less than that lifted clear of the water to windward. This angle of heel which varies from 5–15° according to the strength of the wind and the type of boat, produces an asymmetrical waterline which in itself slightly increases resistance, but this minor disadvantage is far outweighed by the advantages gained by reducing the wetted surface. This asymmetry also produces a tendency to weather helm, and therefore helps to balance the normal tendency to lee helm in very light airs.

Shifting the weight forward also helps to counter the lee helm tendency. This is because the area of lateral resistance, and with it the CLR, move forward. Of course the centreboard must be fully lowered, while in contrast the rudder should not be all the way down. Most dinghies can be steered more accurately and will react quicker if the blade is at an angle of 60–70°. Should the boat still have a slight tendency to lee helm, the rudder can be fully lowered. The combined effect of all these details should leave the dinghy with neutral helm. In very light weather, that is in wind strengths of under Force 1, the angle of heel can be slightly increased to about 20° to help the sail to take up its fullness when the wind is not sufficiently strong to do this.

And this brings us to the tuning of the rig, that is the adjustment and matching of mast to sail. As has already been mentioned in the chapter on rig and sails, theory and practice agree that a sail with an even

curve and central fullness is the most efficient, as regards both pointing and speed. Maximum curvature is no longer in the forward third of the sail but somewhere near the centre, and, although the maximum curvature remains the same, the sail has a smaller angle of entry. The boat can therefore sail a few degrees closer to the wind without the sail lifting. Such a sail has more drive too, especially in light to moderate winds when all the built-in camber can be used. This camber causes the after end of the battens to point up to windward; in other words the leech of a modern sail is more *closed* than that of the old aerofoil type. This is good, for a closed sail produces more power than an open one. The heeling moment is greater, it is true, but that does not matter when the crew's weight is enough to counteract it.

Naturally a foresail cut in this way is also more effective than one with fullness

Left is a modern sail with central camber, right is a sail with the earlier aerofoil section. The maximum depth in the former lies at about 50 per cent, that is exactly in the middle, instead of at 30 per cent back from the mast.

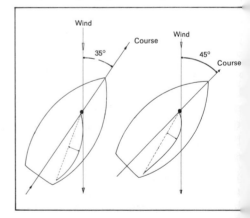

close to the luff, particularly so because there is no thick mast to disturb the airflow along the luff. The rather flatter leading edge results in a lower angle of entry which is all to the good. Here the problems are different, for the foresail is not set on a flexible mast which would be bent forward to flatten the sail. Instead it is set on a length of wire which sags aft and to leeward when under load. The cutting of foresails is critical: the cloth has to be very stable in the bias as all the pressure is concentrated at one point, the clew, but this problem too was resolved not long ago. Modern foresails allow the boat to point extremely high, especially in light winds and smooth waters when the fairlead can be fixed as far inboard as possible to give a very low angle of entry. How far inboard depends primarily on the size and cut of the jib but, in general, the less the jib overlaps the main, the smaller should be the angle. In the International 505 for example, the angle can be as little as 7°. The leech of the jib would then be nearer the centreline of the boat but would backwind the mainsail badly, particularly in the case of a large overlapping genoa like that on a Flying Dutchman. To prevent this the jib must be cut so that it opens well in the upper part of the leech where the slot between mainsail and foresail is particularly narrow. The sailmaker therefore has to ensure that the sail is very stable on the cloth bias in the lower and central area where it comes under heavy load, but much less so in the upper third. It should be obvious that such a sail will only be at its most efficient when used with a modern mainsail with central fullness.

The great advantage in having a jib fairlead which can be adjusted both athwartships and fore-and-aft becomes increasingly obvious. The newer sail shapes are sheeted at different angles from those of older sails. Earlier the fairlead was sited at a point where an imaginary extension of the mitre seam met the deck—now the fairlead is placed further forward, for the jib, like the main, should set in a regular and constant curve. Nevertheless a good foresail will remain open in the upper part of the leech. The foot should be cut deep enough just to brush the deck, so preventing the wind from escaping from the high pressure windward side to the leeward side of the sail, since this would tend to equalise the pressure between the two sides and reduce drive.

To revert to the tuning of the rig after this short digression, in what follows it does not matter what cut of sail is used, a *bird's wing* aerofoil or a sail with central fullness. In both cases in light airs all the available camber of the sail must be used, and this means that the luff of the jib and mainsail, and the foot of the mainsail should be eased until there are no diagonal creases along the boom, the mast or the luff of the jib. In very calm airs other creases may appear which do not matter if they spread out evenly in rays from the fullness in the mainsail. This allows the maximum fullness built into the sail to be used.

The mast should be straight, or possibly

kept as close as possible to the centre line of the boat in spite of a relatively slack mainsheet. This is more effective on those dinghies where the track extends across the full breadth of the transom, than on those with a centre mainsheet. The result will then be that the mainsheet exerts no pressure on the leech, the mast stays relatively straight but the angle of the boom to the centre line, due to the

very slightly bent if the mainsail is extra full, or if a widely overlapping genoa backwinds it. Slightly bending the mast will reduce the depth of fullness by a few centimetres. When beating with a very soft mast, if the mainsheet is sheeted in too hard it will bend the mast too much, and it is better to induce a slight bend by tightening the kicking-strap. A well-hardened mainsheet exerts pressure on the leech which extends to the top of the mast and causes it to bend. The mainsheet, therefore, should only control the angle of the boom upwards.

The athwartships angle can be controlled by using a traveller on a track but fixed to windward so that the boom is

Two ways of adjusting the jib sheet lead in an athwartships direction are shown in these pictures. Above a Fireball with a barber hauler; below a 470 with a track.

A main sheet traveller has its uses in light airs too. By hauling the traveller to windward in spite of the acute angle of the boom to the centreline the sail has a well-opened leech as will be needed at times.

56

traveller being fixed to windward, is small enough to allow the boat to sail as close to the wind as possible, a most important factor in light winds and smooth water. The uppermost batten should be very flexible, and so tensioned in the pocket that it produces a constant curve. Equally, in such light weather, the jib should not be pulled in as stiff as a board either when the sea is flat or when there is a swell.

Gaining the maximum amount of ground to windward is, however, very much dependent on using the right sailing technique. Absolute stillness in the boat is more important than is often thought. Every unnecessary and jerky movement is transmitted to the sails causing them to lift, and also affects the laminar flow of water past the bottom which should be uninterrupted, particularly in these

weather conditions. The helmsman should avoid using the helm violently and should alter course as sensitively and smoothly as possible. The same holds good when going about, for the rudder need only follow the boat's reactions. If a boat is heeled a bit more she will go about of her own accord. An ability to concentrate

Without a traveller to bring the boom close amidships hardening in the mainsheet would close the sail leech too much.

Here everything is right—weight forward, slight heel, an almost straight mast and boom. This photo was taken in about Force 1½.

and to be observant in light airs plays no less important a rôle than sensitive steering, correct tuning and balance, for it is just such weather that produces frequent wind shifts.

A boat will point best in smooth water, and this means delicate steering, for with the flat leading edges of the new sail shapes it is only too easy to sail too close and pinch without realising it because the luff of the jib does not lift so easily. If there is some sea or a swell the sheets should be eased slightly, for it is then even more important to have maximum camber in a *closed* sail so that power will build up, and increased power is needed to overcome the effect of waves smacking against the hull. When easing sheets care should be taken that the motion of the boat's hull is not transferred to the sails causing them to slat. Easing sheets will mean that the boat points less well, but this is more than compensated for by the increase in speed and the reduction in leeway.

This boat is well trimmed for moderate wind speeds and smooth waters. The mast is curved gently over its whole length by sheeting in the boom fairly hard. (Near right.)

And this is how the sails look from aft. Already the upper half of the leech is open even in this lightish wind, as happens particularly with tall narrow mainsails. (Far right.)

58

Beating in Moderate Winds

When the wind increases to Force 2 or 3, in other words to a strength which still does not call for the use of the trapeze, other dynamic forces come to the fore which naturally affect the trim of the boat. Gradually the importance of reducing the wetted surface fades. Instead the dinghy should be sailed upright, that is at an angle of not more than 5° of heel, with the weight concentrated about the boat's centre of gravity amidships. The centreboard, as before, remains fully lowered, but should the dinghy have some weather helm it can be raised slightly so that the tip moves slightly aft which also causes the CLR to shift slightly aft to balance

the CE. The rudder will be right down because, due to the increase in speed, the boat will answer the helm perfectly without the necessity for increased leverage.

As to the rig, it will now be seen whether the mast really matches the sail. The boom, which should be fairly stiff, can now be hardened in by the mainsheet, for the apparent wind strikes at a narrower angle to the centre line due to the increased speed, and this calls for a narrowing of the angle of the main boom. The jib, too, can be trimmed in more and the fairlead shifted slightly further aft, that is approximately to the point where the imaginary extension of the mitre meets the deck, or if there is no mitre, the line which divides the angle of the clew.

The close-hauled boom tensions the chord of the leech and this increases the bend in the mast. The mast should bend more at the top, both sideways and aft,

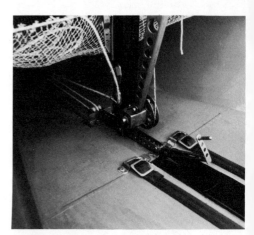

Nowadays mast controls at deck level are among the most important fittings in light displacement dinghies. In the Fireball on the left there is a short tackle which runs through two cheek blocks on the deck and two clam cleats. To hold the mast straighter the tackle is tightened.

One of the most up-to-date screw adjusters for the heel of the mast. (Top.)

Below is a mast control on a 470.

but the degree of bend in the lower two-thirds needs to be controlled to allow the sail to take up the variety of shapes that are needed in different conditions and moderate winds. Wooden chocks are the simplest form of control in plywood dinghies. They can be inserted forward of the mast where it passes through the deck to limit the degree of bend, or can be removed to allow it to bend fully. Fibreglass dinghies with more or less

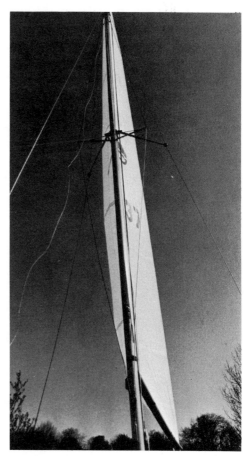

If the wind increases to Force 2 or 3 the luff and foot must be tautened, otherwise the luff will wrinkle as in the upper picture when the boom is sheeted in. The amount of camber is controlled by the luff, and just how much flatter a sail becomes with only moderate tightening of the luff tension,

and no other alterations to the rig, can be seen in the two lower photos.

free-standing masts usually have some form of leverage system whereby a tackle or a lever controls the degree of mast bend. The length on which leverage is exerted is relatively small by comparison with the remaining mast length, so that even a slight adjustment will have a big effect and this should not be underrated. Where a mast is very soft the lower two-thirds must be kept well under control so that it does not bend too much. It should not be forgotten that spreaders and bending controls must work reciprocally. In contrast to the spreaders, mast bend controls can be adjusted while sailing.

The general trend today is towards stiffer masts so that hardening the mainsheet will normally cause the right amount of bend. The increase in wind pressure means that the leech will stretch to become more open and not curve back against the wind so much. It is not enough just to get the right degree of mast bend, for it will immediately be seen that the whole of the sail is pulled into long diagonal creases from boom to mast. The tension of the various edges of the sail must therefore be adjusted to agree with the amount of bend in the mast and the pressure of the wind. As the curvature of a sail is controlled largely by the tension of the luff, the jib should be dealt with by tightening the luff downhaul and the mainsail by pulling down the goose-neck until these folds disappear. The tension of the foot of the mainsail should also be increased.

An alternative method of tensioning the luff of the mainsail is by means of the Cunningham hole. This is a cringle sewn into the sail 10–25 cm. above the tack, or sometimes a block is sewn to the sail instead of the cringle to reduce friction. The tension of the luff can then easily be altered while under way by pulling down the Cunningham hole. The alternative method of pulling down the goose-neck can be very hard and also affects the kicking-strap setting. Creases will appear in the sail when the Cunningham hole is used, but these do not matter because they appear in the area where there is a lot of turbulence in any case due to the junction of the mast and boom. In winds of up to Force 3, the mast is tuned to make use of the whole available camber of a mainsail, and the maximum depth of chord remains in the middle of the sail. Above this wind force the sail is gradually flattened by bending the mast more.

With regard to sailing technique, the crew should concentrate their weight in the middle of the boat, preferably close together to minimise wind resistance. The helmsman should sit as far forward as possible while still being able to steer efficiently using the tiller extension, for suction at the transom is to be avoided in this sort of weather too to encourage the boat to slip more easily through the waves. Heeling must be avoided for not only does it cause a reduction in speed due to increased weather helm, but the area of lateral resistance is reduced and the boat will make more leeway. Variations in wind strength can mostly be countered by sitting out in the normal way using toe-straps. The boat will now point really high, except where larger waves have developed, in which case the traveller can be allowed to slide further to leeward and the boat sailed rather freer. As has already been stated, in rough weather what is needed is speed through the waves rather than concentration on pointing as high as possible.

This boat is being sailed perfectly in a moderate breeze. The crew are sitting close together in the centre of the boat and she is sailing fast and almost upright and with neutral helm. The sails, which are still set to be full, are producing maximum drive. The wire strops between the main sheet blocks and the boom shorten the quantity of rope needed.

Beating in a Strong Wind

The trim of the boat in heavy weather should be obvious. Above all the dinghy should be sailed as upright as possible, though never at the cost of speed. The effect of an increased angle of heel has already been mentioned: the reduction in the area of lateral resistance and the simultaneous increase in weather helm result in an increased braking effect from using the rudder to counteract weather helm, while a lot of leeway is made which not only means loss of ground to windward but also reduced speed. Centreboard and rudder, therefore, stay fully down unless the crew intend to half plane. If this were the object the crew would not keep their weight in the middle of the boat but, as when planing with the wind free, would move further aft. The centreboard should then be raised slightly because the area of lateral resistance is of lesser importance at increased speeds. This also brings the CLR further aft and thus reduces weather helm.

The basic principle when beating in a strong wind is: the stronger the wind, the flatter and more *open* the sail should be. And that can only happen when the mast is flexible enough to match the character of the mainsail. To put it simply, the mast must pull as much fullness out of the sail as is necessary for the crew to be able to hold the dinghy upright. It is essential that the sail should keep its optimum shape without developing creases or losing wind. As already mentioned, fullness in the sail brings increased power and

This is the way to do it in strong winds. The crew are in perfect positions and are close together at the boat's centre of gravity which, in these conditions, lies just aft of amidships. The dinghy is nicely balanced, is upright, and travelling

64

*ery fast. The helmsman is holding the tiller extension with
only two fingers, and obviously has to exert no pressure on
the rudder to hold this course.*

65

Although the traveller is fixed amidships, the crew has the boat under good control. This sail opens well at the top, partly because of its tall narrow shape.

This Flying Dutchman crew are sailing the boat in typical heavy weather tune, although the bend of the mast is not yet extreme. But for today's stiff booms, the bend in this boom would already be at its maximum.

enables a boat to point higher in light airs but, as the wind increases, fullness also increases the angle of heel, and if the crew are unable to counter this by using their weight the result will be a loss in speed and less ground gained to windward.

The general tendency today is towards 'flatter sails with smooth curves set on stiffer masts' but that does not alter the fact that modern arc-shaped sails, even when flattened, produce not only greater drive but also greater side force and therefore greater heeling moment. The higher up the sail the heeling moment

occurs in the sail, the greater the leverage on the boat and consequently the greater the angle of heel. This can only be counteracted by a sail with a leech that opens in stronger winds thus allowing the wind to exhaust easily and reduce the heeling moment. The skill of the sailmaker lies in cutting a sail with a leech that will open progressively from top to bottom when suitably trimmed. Obviously a sail should open first where the heeling moment is greatest in proportion to drive, right up high in the sail. This will happen when the mast bends properly, and that means that the mast must bend more up

If an averagely stiff mast has no limiting staying (like this Fireball) the lower parts bend too much forward and to windward in stronger winds, and that can only be due to the heavy forward push of the boom.

The same can also happen if the spreaders are not properly adjusted as in this photo. The result is a thoroughly distorted sail shape which has lost much of its drive.

high than in the lower two thirds. The lower part of the mast should only bend as much as the wind pressure necessitates, that is, enough to allow the crew to keep the boat upright.

In brief: the greater the heeling moment, the more fullness should be taken out of the sail progressively from top to bottom. Because the lowest third of the sail produces most drive in proportion to heeling moment, this part of the sail should always be trimmed to be at its most effective, and the leech here should therefore remain closed when it is already open higher up.

This is one reason for having a relatively stiff boom, for a flexible one does just what it should not; by pulling down in the centre where the mainsheet is attached it removes fullness from the lower part of the sail, while the end of the boom simultaneously pulls upwards and to leeward allowing the leech to open. The opposite case, a boom which rises in the centre and droops at the end is even worse. This often happens in dinghies with a sheet lead running from the transom to the end of the boom, and although a centre sheet lead has proved itself to be more practical and efficient over the years, there are still a good many dinghies around with stern mainsheet leads.

So in practice, this is what should happen: in Force 4 and above, the luff and foot of the main and the luff of the jib are fully tensioned. The jib fairlead is positioned in line with the imaginary extension of the mitre, or perhaps a little further aft if the wind is such that a more open leech is needed. The tauter luff and foot of the mainsail, together with the right degree of mast bend, flatten the sail and open the leech. The tauter edges of the sail also discourage the camber from moving aft of the centre of the sail.

At the top the mast must be flexible enough to bend well to leeward and aft,

so that the upper third of the leech can open freely. That reduces the heeling moment considerably, but affects the drive relatively little. The stronger the wind becomes, and the less able the crew is to hold the dinghy upright, the further down must the leech open. This is done by increasing forward bend in the lower two-thirds of the mast, that is from the fore-stay attachment down, which not only flattens the camber but simultaneously allows the leech to open.

With a stiff mast that does not bend enough, the easiest way to get the necessary degree of bend is by using spreaders under compression angled aft. With a

The mast should only bend to leeward above the jib stay which allows the sail first to open in the upper leech area as is wanted in increasing winds.

68

flexible mast that bends too much initially, spreaders under tension will prevent excessive bending. If diamonds are rigged it is possible to prevent sideways bending of the mast if they are angled slightly forward. The central part of the mast can be controlled to a certain degree in a fore-and-aft direction as well. The disadvantages of diamonds have been explained. They hold the whole mast too rigid thereby restricting its ability to absorb the shock of the waves. Mast bend controls regulate the bending of the mast in a fore-and-aft direction and should always be used in conjunction with the spreaders. As the spreaders cannot be altered under

In single-handed dinghies like the Finn the leverage of a trapeze hand is missing. Therefore, even in Force 3 winds and over, the traveller has to be allowed to drop to leeward. Finn sailors have to be very strong and fit.

Below the forestay the mast should only bend forwards and not to one side. If the mast is too stiff and does not bend forward, the same thing will happen as is seen here. The sail is too full, is backwinded, and in a strong wind can lose its shape completely. The leech of the jib is closed too much also.

way, mast bend controls are used to make the finer adjustments.

It is not until the weather becomes really fierce that the lowest third of the leech is allowed to open, and this is brought about by bending the lower part of the mast strongly. The mast bend control is used for this, with a very tightly set up kicking-strap. If that is not enough the main sheet blocks can be moved further aft along the boom to increase the forward pressure on the mast. The position is often reached when the mast bends more than the fullness of the sail allows, and this results in creases running out from the end of the boom like rays. The degree of bend of the mast no longer matches the shape of the sail because all the fullness has already been flattened out.

But sailing in these conditions demands real specialist techniques. The crew now

has the additional problem of sailing the dinghy as upright as possible by countering the pressure of the wind with lightning fast reactions and agility. Weight must be as far out as possible for as long as possible with the trapeze artist standing in a comfortable harness at an angle of 85–90° to the mast, while the helmsman, using toe-straps adjusted to the correct height, sits out in the least tiring but as effective a position as possible. In order to keep wind resistance small they should be close one behind the other and at the boat's centre of gravity. Just where depends to a certain extent on how the boat is to be sailed. If, as is more and more practised, the aim is to half-plane on the beat, then the forward part of the boat must be lightened and the crew will sit further aft to concentrate the centre of gravity there. This method is especially recommended for lightly-built dinghies with a comparatively heavy crew who can still manage to hold the boat upright. If the boat is to be sailed on a normal close-hauled course, particularly with heavier dinghies, then the centre of gravity should lie slightly aft of the centre of the boat.

Half-planing is most advantageous when beating in a sea, for waves build up at approximately right angles to the direction of the wind, and if the boat points too high her bow will cut more directly into

*If easing sheets in gusts in unavoidable, it should be the main-
sail that is eased rather than the jib, for otherwise weather
helm is increased as the CE of the wind pressure shifts further
aft.*

them and she will slow down. By bearing
away slightly and by simultaneously shifting the weight a little further aft, the angle
is improved and the bow lifts more easily
to the waves with a considerable increase
in speed. If one or several particularly
big waves loom, it is best to point the
dinghy really high and reduce her speed
so that she can lift more easily to them.

*This photo demonstrates classically how important it is to
keep the boat level in a strong wind. The angle of heel causes
a sudden decrease in the area of lateral plane which makes
for a lot of leeway, and that not only means loss of ground
to windward but also loss of speed, because the increased
wind pressure is not converted into sufficient forward drive.*

When the waves are back to normal bear away again to regain maximum speed. It is particularly important to trim the jib and the mainsail to the same angle in heavy weather, and this is one of the reasons why helmsman and crew should be well used to each other in boisterous conditions. Obviously a relatively quiet patch of water should be picked in which to make a tack.

With regard to sail trimming, it is a question of playing the mainsheet and traveller constantly. In dinghies with no traveller, a well-hardened down kicking strap can be a partial substitute, but this is more awkward to trim. When the crew is out on the wire he can only alter the tension of the kicking strap while going about, whereas the angle of the mainsail can be continuously adjusted by playing the mainsheet and traveller. It is therefore necessary to find the best, but ever-varying compromise between easing sheets slightly and dropping the traveller off to leeward.

In a heavy sea, if the currently popular method is adopted of hauling the sheets in pretty tight and slacking the traveller in gusts, the same effect is felt as with tight diamonds. The mast loses its elasticity and cannot adjust to the movement of the boat, causing the dinghy to pound and slow down in the waves. The sail will also

The technique of half planing on the beat is practised by practically all modern racing dinghies, particularly when there are waves. The weight distribution should be like this.

be too flat which leads to a loss of power and, remember a powerful sail is more important in a seaway than a sail trimmed purely for speed. So a convenient compromise, which is and in any case only to be found by trial and error, must be reached so that the mast can to a certain extent cushion the effect of the waves. As a rule of thumb, where there are many large waves the sheet should be eased more and the traveller less, while the opposite should be the case where there is less sea. Further, if the dinghy suffers from heavy weather helm, the traveller should not be allowed to drop to leeward.

Capsizes occur relatively rarely when beating and are avoidable as, even in strong winds, the dinghy can be kept well under control. The critical moment comes when there are violent gusts as on inland waters, or where the wind comes from the land off steep coasts. Then it is necessary to bear away at lightning speed in the lulls to avoid going for a swim to windward. Finally, the boat can point higher in the gusts because the wind then frees appreciably due to the increase in speed of the true wind in relation to the apparent wind.

When half planing, bear away slightly, whereupon the bow cuts the waves at a better angle. Otherwise the boat will slam hard into each wave with consequent loss of speed and increased leeway. As the picture shows, this also means more spray!

This dinghy is 'in irons' and drifting backwards. The helms‑
man is despairingly trying to put his boat on to the starboar
tack by putting the helm hard over, and the crew is thinkin
he is still going forward already sheeting in the jib, whic
is wrong in any case. In such a situation there is only on
thing to do: the helmsman should pull in the mainsail an
keep his rudder amidships until the dinghy goes astern an
takes up a course on either the new or old tack. This happer
mainly in strong winds before the start of a race, or whe
tacking and the boat has not enough way on. When goin
about it is better to bear away slightly and then put he
round quickly, preferably not where there is a particular
large wave. It is better not to do the same as the Flyir
Dutchman (left). Here the crew is already starting to ha
the jib in on the new tack before the bows have passed throug
the wind. He should wait until the bow is head to wind whe
the jib will want to cross over of its own accord.

TUNING AND SAILING
TECHNIQUE REACHING

If beating calls for a compromise between pointing as high as possible and maintaining maximum speed, at least sailing with the wind free is easier in that the sole aim is speed. No other considerations have to be taken into account such as the gaining of ground to windward when beating. This means that, in light and moderate winds at least, there are fewer but more subtle ways of reaching a destination more quickly than other people. Above a certain wind strength, however, when conditions are right for planing, the chances of increasing speed are all the greater, for dinghies will now be sailing at their fastest. The difference between good and very good sailing technique can result in a gain of 50–100 metres in a few minutes. Naturally correct trim and tuning plays an important part, but this is relatively small by comparison with the effects of correct handling technique. It is true that it is virtually impossible to describe in a few abstract sentences what basically is a matter of feel and intuition and which, together with the necessary talent, needs years of experience. Therefore the paragraphs on technique which accompany hints on trim and tuning are only ideas on which to build as a result of experience.

Reaching in Light Airs

Reduce the wetted surface—that is still the essential when reaching in light breezes. So, weight must be kept well forward until the transom is clear of the water, and the dinghy should be slightly heeled. The centreboard and rudder can be almost half way up, rather further up on a broad reach than on a close reach.

Adjustments to the rig are not particularly complicated. The mast should be straight and the luff and the foot of the mainsail as well as the luff of the jib should be slackened until the sails are as full as possible. When on a very close reach the luff of the main can even have small diagonal folds. The jib fairlead is either directly in line with the extension of the mitre, or else slightly forward of this point

Some crews prefer to trim the spinnaker from the trapeze even in light airs, which consequently means that the helmsman must sit to leeward. Conversely some helmsmen prefer to sit to leeward which means that the jib hand has to use the trapeze. Using this technique you can not only trim the spinnaker better but also improve the balance of the boat.

in very light airs. The main sheet traveller is right to leeward of the track, and the kicking-strap only lightly tensioned.

Sailing technique is rather more complicated, particularly if the spinnaker is set. If there is no spinnaker the jib and mainsail should be eased out as far as possible until the luffs are almost lifting. If the spinnaker is set, mainsail and jib should be hardened in slightly, especially on a close reach, for otherwise they will be backwinded by the spinnaker. The jib should still be carried provided that it is drawing reasonably well. Only if the wind is very light, say under Force 1, should the jib be furled or tied up with a light line. Furling gear can be very advantageous as

it is then possible to leave the last third set.

When reaching in light airs, the helmsman will almost always sit to leeward and the crew forward of the shroud to windward so as to control the spinnaker boom directly with the guy, for he can then trim it more accurately and sensitively than with a spinnaker boom downhaul hooked on. He should let the boom ride high so that the luff slightly accentuates the flow in the spinnaker, and should play the spinnaker sheet with his other hand, easing it until the luff of the spinnaker is just short of collapsing. On a close reach the spinnaker does not simply push the boat to leeward but gives real forward

This boat is well trimmed for such calm conditions. The weight is forward and she is slightly heeled, the rudder blade is lifted a little, while the furled jib does not disturb the flow of air to the spinnaker which is drawing well although it being used near to its limit of close reaching.

drive.

To decide when the flat cut spinnakers currently in use produce more drive than the jib alone is a problem that can only be resolved by experience, for there are several factors involved, the most important of which are the shape and stability of the boat, the strength of the wind, the cut of the spinnaker and, of course, the experience and ability of the crew. The borderline varies by about 10°, and a course 60° to the wind is usually the highest at which a spinnaker can be carried and then only in light winds. Normally with a big overlapping genoa as in the Flying Dutchman class, the spinnaker will be lowered earlier than where the jib is small. For guidance it can be suggested that the spinnaker should be lowered when the spinnaker boom is touching the forestay and the sheet has to be hardened in so much that the foot of the spinnaker is under tension which restricts the flow. In such a borderline case it is much better first to bear away a little with the spinnaker set, when it will produce more drive than the jib alone, and then to lower the spinnaker and point higher for the second half of the leg under jib and mainsail alone. When reaching in light winds, steer as sensitively and gently as possible, and keep still.

Reaching in Moderate Winds

General rules for trimming the boat: weight should be far enough forward to prevent the transom dragging through the water: the angle of heel should be

In these conditions the jib can well be left set providing the boat has not got a widely overlapping genoa like a Flying Dutchman. If in doubt, the further the jib overlaps, the earlier should it be lowered.

reduced so that the dinghy sails nearly upright: the centreboard should be at an angle of 40–50° and the rudder should be lowered to about 60°.

Tuning the rig in this weather is also relatively simple. The mast should be bent slightly along its whole length by tightening the kicking-strap, so that camber of the mainsail is reduced by a few centimetres to prevent its being backwinded by the spinnaker on a close reach. The edges of the sails should still be slack, though not quite so slack as in lighter airs. The jib sheet lead lies in line with the extension of the mitre, and the mainsheet traveller right to leeward.

As to sailing technique, there are some who already have a trick or two up their sleeves. For example, how to get a dinghy to plane in a bare Force 3 wind. This is primarily a question of effective co-ordination of helmsman and crew, and in this case the crew has the more important rôle to play, for only perfect spinnaker drill combined with rhythmic movement will enable a dinghy to lift out of normal displacement sailing into a plane.

This is how it goes. Already hooked on to the trapeze wire the crew sits on the windward deck holding the sheet in one hand and the guy in the other, with the spinnaker boom set with a slight upward tilt by means of the uphaul and downhaul. The helmsman begins to luff gently and pulls the main sheet a little tighter which causes the dinghy to heel slightly, while the crew trims the spinnaker carefully, his weight on the wire but still in a crouching position. What follows occurs simultaneously. The crew stretches out hauling in on both guy and sheet while the helmsman bears away with a jerk, and both move their weight further aft to lift the bow. At that moment, when the dinghy bears away and comes upright, these different factors combine to lift the dinghy out of normal sailing up into a plane. Planing can then be maintained by rhythmic bearing away and luffing if there is good co-ordination between helmsman and crew.

When racing it would be possible, for example, to gain half the length of the reach in this way when other boats could

The most effective position for a spinnaker is always a compromise between easing the lee sheet considerably and hauling aft on the guy. Ideas are often very different (see picture). G 1022 looks best here.

78

not be lifted into a plane, and light crews would be at an advantage here. In races this technique is all too often performed blatantly, and is then frequently interpreted as 'pumping' which is expressly forbidden by the racing rules. It is therefore necessary either to contrive a less obvious method, or else practise it purely for pleasure. It is, however, most advantageous and thoroughly legitimate to use this technique in borderline wind strengths to get a dinghy to start to plane. If there is no chance of planing, the boat should be sailed much the same as in light airs, but almost upright.

This boat could be planing in this Force 3 breeze. Then the crew would have to move further aft. The sails need to be trimmed more sensitively, for the spinnaker here is angled far too close to the wind, as the eased out mainsail shows.

The 505 above has unusually pronounced mast bend reaching in winds of Force 3 to 4.

Reaching in Strong Winds

It follows logically that the dinghy should be sailed as upright as possible in strong winds, and that the bow should be lifted out of the water, for planing conditions prevail. So weight should be aft. An often exaggerated tendency to weather helm and the upright sailing position together mean that to raise the centreboard only slightly is not enough. The correct angle for the centreboard is 45° which shifts the CLR further aft, and this is only possible because at speed a boat makes virtually no leeway. In contrast the rudder should be right down in a vertical position.

So as to avoid being overpowered, the luff and foot of the mainsail and the luff of the jib must be tautened almost as much as for a hard beat. In really hard weather there is no need to take the trouble to ease the tension a touch when reaching, for under these conditions the boat is sailing at maximum speed anyway. The mast must bend more to match, and as the normal method of doing this by pulling downwards hard on the mainsheet is not so effective due to the angle of the boom outboard, the bend will not be, and should not be, quite so pronounced as on a close beat.

A really tight kicking-strap combined with suitably adjusted spreaders and mast control will produce the desired amount of bend. The kicking-strap also prevents the boom lifting and is the guarantee of as flat a mainsail as possible for, except

This crew demonstrates ideal boat trim for a fast reach. The bow is out of the water back to the mast, and the jib hand is balancing the boat so that she is on an absolutely even keel.

81

on close reaches, the boom is at such a broad angle outboard that the pull of the sheet from a traveller set right to leeward will pull the main boom in rather than down. The kicking-strap, therefore, plays a very important rôle.

Correct sailing technique on fast reaches not only yields the greatest speed and most excitement, but is also the hardest to achieve, especially with a spinnaker set. The crew must rely largely on feel to decide when the boat is perfectly trimmed and at the most efficient planing angle, for only then will she sail at maximum speed. The best place for weight distribution must be found by experiment and the helmsman must play the mainsheet continuously to help the trapeze hand's efforts to keep the boat upright. As far as possible it is important that easing or hardening in the jib and main sheets should occur in unison, and that again is

to a large degree dependent upon how well the helmsman and crew work together. To avoid an unnecessary increase in dead weight as a result of spray collecting in the bottom, where the boat has a solid transom, self-bailers and transom flaps should be left open. In very gusty winds a fast reach is a matter of continuous luffing and bearing away. When a gust strikes the helmsman bears away and eases the mainsheet, while the crew in the trapeze simultaneously pulls the spinnaker to windward to keep it as free as possible from the turbulence of the jib, so that it produces maximum drive. Under these conditions the jib is usually left drawing, cleated at an average angle, so that the crew can concentrate on trimming the spinnaker.

The downhaul should keep the spinnaker boom slightly raised so that the luff is not tight but allows the spinnaker enough fullness to be most effective. In hard winds, too, a good crew on the wire will not only try to prevent the spinnaker collapsing but attempt to keep it clear of the turbulence of the jib by easing the sheet as much as possible until the luff is on the point of *breaking*. He can, of course, do this most effectively if he can hold the guy in one hand and the sheet in the other, for he can then find the ideal balance between easing the sheet considerably and pulling back the guy. This is hard work, however, and demands such physical fitness that the average crew cannot cope.

On fast reaches the mast should bend slightly forward along the whole of its length (more so on close reaches than on beam reaches) but should be stiff sideways.

This dinghy is sailing the same course without a spinnaker and is moving much better.

The photo on the next pages also shows a 505. The crew should have their weight further aft to bring the bow more out of the water. The mainsail is flattened by a tightly set up kicking-strap and therefore is producing maximum drive. The spinnaker boom should not be pressing on the forestay.

If the wind is not too gusty or changeable in direction, the guy can be made fast so that the boom is fixed in a position which allows the spinnaker to draw most effectively whatever course the boat is on. In boats with large genoas the boom on a close reach should always be at least a hand's breadth away from the forestay.

When a gust strikes, the helmsman should bear away very quickly and both helmsman and crew must use their weight to keep the boat as upright as possible. The gust will not only be better absorbed in this way, but will also be made use of

for longer by running with it. Stay on this course as long as the dinghy is still planing fast in the gust. When it eases the mainsail and spinnaker can be hardened in and the boat luffed, for fortunately on a reach the boat is not as closely restricted to a specific course as when beating. By gently luffing up to the average course or even above it the boat can be kept planing as long as possible, for the sails can then be trimmed close enough to benefit from a more laminar airstream which then produces the greater drive, provided that the crew can still keep the dinghy upright. Naturally

Here the helmsman has not reacted quickly enough to a gust. The dinghy is out of control and heeling violently. The crew has panicked and let the jib sheet fly. If the gust now

eases there is danger of capsizing to windward unless the crew gets back aboard quickly. Another point—being barefoot on the trapeze is dangerous and it is easy to get hurt.

this is largely a question of feel, and the man who has that will pull well ahead in races, even on those legs of a course where practically everybody is sailing in the same direction. The best planing technique is always decisive here, but to that must be added quick reactions to approaching gusts. If the helmsman does not bear away immediately, the dinghy will be pressed sideways, heel violently and suffer a lot of weather helm, and then all sheets will have to be eased before she can bear away.

If no spinnaker is hoisted, and Force 6 to 7 is the maximum for even the best of crews, the same things should be done under mainsail and jib alone, with the sheets being eased and hardened in simultaneously as far as is possible. To summarise: when sailing on a fast reach the dinghy must under all circumstances be sailed as upright as possible, with the sails sheeted at the angle which will produce the most drive. When gusts strike which are heavy enough to call for a reduction of sail area by easing main, jib and spinnaker sheets, bear away quickly instead. This also entails easing sheets, it is true,

In this picture the helmsman has borne away at lightning speed and caught the gust well to run with it at increased speed. By trimming the weight aft the crew has lightened the fore part of the boat. The mainsail should, however, be flatter which could be done by tightening the kicking-strap.

but only as the boat is bearing away which means that the angle of the sail to the wind does not alter, and nor does the area of the sail being used. The increased wind pressure is therefore converted into increased boat speed. The greater heeling moment which would normally put the boat on her ears is converted into increased forward drive, and the more the boat's bow is turned away from the wind, the more wind can she stand, for the power will act more forward and she will sail faster. Similarly, when the gust eases, point higher to increase the apparent wind and establish laminar airflow. Greatest speed will only be achieved when wind pressure can be exactly balanced by weight of crew.

This boat is sailing at full speed in a very hard squall. The crew have their weight far aft and have borne away on to a course on which the boat can best cope with this gust.

TUNING AND SAILING
TECHNIQUE RUNNING

As on a reach, when the wind is dead aft all adjustments and effort go towards increasing speed. No other considerations need be considered such as pointing high on a beat. In fact, there is here an opposite factor to think about, namely whether to increase the distance sailed if this benefits overall speed. When the course is a run a boat is hardly ever sailed with the wind dead aft. One of the reasons is that the modern cut spinnaker produces maximum drive in laminar airstreams, i.e. when air flows across it. Additionally a fully eased mainsail, as is necessary with the wind aft, can never be at the correct angle to the wind, for the boom is bound to come up against the shroud at an angle of about 80°. Again, the jib draws better with the wind about on the quarter. All these cir-

This spinnaker is flying free and unhindered by the turbulence of the mainsail. The guy is pulled well back far to windward and the lee sheet is eased as far as possible. The spinnaker is set at its most effective point.

Total calm reigns and the crews have their weight well forward and to leeward. Here the angle of heel helps the sails to drop into shape.

cumstances taken together result in the fact that today modern light displacement dinghies practically always sail the running leg of a course at angles of 75–80° to the wind. Only under true planing conditions, if at all, does the direct route pay. Naturally this way of sailing downwind means a slight increase in the distance sailed and at least one gybe, but the enormous increase in speed outweighs these disadvantages.

Running in Light Winds

Again the boat should be trimmed so that the wetted surface is reduced by keeping weight forward and heeling the boat slightly. The lateral area can now be reduced by lifting the centreboard almost entirely. Only about ten centimetres should protrude to give directional stability through the water. The rudder blade should be at an angle of 60–70°.

With regard to the rig, the mast should be straight in the position it would take up naturally before being deliberately bent. The mainsail, as on other courses, should be hoisted as high as possible with the head at the upper limit band, for the speed of the wind high up is greater than just above the surface of the water. The jib sheet lead, unless the jib is furled, lies in line with the extension of the mitre, and the mainsheet traveller should be right to leeward. The luff and foot of the mainsail, and the luff of the jib should be eased to give the sails maximum camber.

It has been proved by experience that a mast which leans slightly forward makes a boat run slightly faster. On modern dinghies such as the Flying Dutchman, increasingly these days the shrouds are led through the deck to drum winches or

The luff of the mainsail on Vaurien G. 23397 has been slackened too far, and this is causing the diagonal folds. So long as the boat is sailing almost dead before the wind this does not matter, but if she luffs only slightly to the point where laminar airflow begins a sail like that of G. 23414 will be much more effective.

The Flying Dutchman above is being sailed well, and with sails correctly trimmed, for a dead run.

92

levers so that they can be eased under way. Lengthening the shrouds allows the whole rig to lean further forward. If it is not possible to make such an adjustment, the mast should at least stand as straight as possible and avoid a rake aft.

As to sailing technique, once again it is a question of stillness in the boat, gentle and sensitive steering, and attentive observation. The boom is let out until it gently touches the shroud. The jib should be furled or tied up with a line because in a light wind it can add nothing in the way of drive and instead will disturb the flow of air from the spinnaker. Further, the crew can then concentrate entirely on keeping the spinnaker full when gybing. While the helmsman sits on the leedeck, the crew is best sited on the foredeck with the spinnaker guy in one hand and the sheet in the other, so that he can control the sail better and more sensitively in very light and variable winds. The luff should be very slack to give extra fullness to the spinnaker and should under no circumstances come under tension.

The crew's problem is to find the most effective compromise between easing the sheet considerably and pulling back the guy—the one always affects the other. If the sheet is eased a lot, then the spinnaker will lift beautifully and will fly more or less abeam well away from the mainsail but still in its turbulent zone. On the other hand if the spinnaker guy is pulled back so that the boom is further to windward free from turbulence from the main, the wind will then be clearer but the spinnaker cannot lift so much as the sheet has to be pulled in more.

It is possible to gybe without allowing the spinnaker to fall in if the helmsman trims the sheets while the spinnaker boom is transferred. The crew can stop the spinnaker collapsing by pushing the pole sideways as the boom gybes over and at the same time the helmsman trims the new spinnaker sheet.

Gybing normally goes like this: both spinnaker sheet and guy are made fast and, while the helmsman gently and gradually bears away passing the mainsail to the other side, the crew unhooks the spinnaker boom from the mast and attaches it to the new tack of the spinnaker. He then detaches the other end from the spinnaker and hooks it onto the mast. The helmsman immediately uncleats the new spinnaker sheet and hauls it in to prevent the spinnaker from collapsing along the luff. Once the spinnaker boom has been hooked on, he hands the sheet back to the crew. Ever lighter and thinner sheets are being used in light airs. It must be obvious that the jib should be unfurled before lowering the spinnaker and luffing up.

Running in Moderate Winds

There is no longer any need for the gentle angle of heel, and the dinghy should be sailed upright. The weight of the crew should remain far enough forward to allow the water to stream aft smoothly. The centreboard need only be lowered about 15 cm. and the rudder blade should be at an angle of 45°.

So far as the rig is concerned, the kicking-strap should be tightened to give slight mast bend along the whole length. The kicking-strap is needed anyway to stop the boom lifting and the sail distorting. The luff and foot of the mainsail and the luff of the jib should still be slack, and slight diagonal creases are permissible along the luff of the mainsail. The jib

sheet lead stays in the extension of the mitre line, and the traveller to leeward.

Sailing technique under these conditions gives fewest opportunities of gaining big advantages in races. Technique is simple so that even untrained crews can quickly acquire the necessary skills. Even so there are little subtleties which can win an extra metre or two, for example when setting the spinnaker. This is relatively easy in boats with a spinnaker chute, but more tricky in boats without one.

Care should be taken to hoist the spinnaker to leeward of the jib, which under these weather conditions will be pulling quite well and should therefore be left standing. It is then quite simple for the crew to control the spinnaker which will be bellying out to leeward, by hardening

The trim of this Finn is faultless. She is sailing upright and with neutral helm. However the boom is lifting slightly too much which reduces the sail area presented to the wind from aft.

in the sheet and at the same time hooking the end of the boom to the spinnaker to windward and thus have it drawing in a few seconds. In this way there is no friction and no possibility of getting tangled up, for the spinnaker can fly freely out to leeward of the other sails while being set.

On the other hand, if it is hoisted to windward there is the danger that the crew may not pull the sheet in at the right moment to get the sail round to leeward of the jib, and then that part of the spinnaker which has not blown to leeward can fill with wind and press into the jib. It will then be very difficult to get it clear to leeward. If there is no alternative to hoisting the spinnaker to windward, and in races this does happen, then the crew

must take care to pull hard on the sheet while the helmsman is hoisting the spinnaker, and so pull the sail round to the lee side of the forestay before it fills. It always pays on a run, however, to lower the spinnaker to windward. On a reach always pull the spinnaker in by the clew having let the guy go at the same time.

In moderate winds the spinnaker boom will be held in the right position by means of a downhaul. The guy can be cleated, provided the wind is not too fluky. The crew, who will be sitting on the windward deck about level with the shrouds, will only have the sheet to trim, which he should ease as far as possible without collapsing the luff of the spinnaker. The rule here is the same: the spinnaker must

The spinnaker should already open and start to draw while it is being set. This can happen if the crew trims the sheet with one hand while, with the other, he guides the spinnaker boom into its clip after it is attached to the tack. This is

not happening here, for the spinnaker sheets are free and dragging in the water and they are likely to get tangled up.

be kept free of the turbulence of the other sails, and again a compromise must be reached between a well-eased sheet and a boom pulled back to windward.

The helmsman eases the mainsail until the boom lightly touches the shrouds, while the jib which is usually trimmed by the helmsman will be sheeted at a rather closer angle than the direction of the wind demands. The dinghy, as we have already heard, is not sailed dead before the wind but at an angle of some 10° to one side of it.

Running in Strong Winds

Trimming the boat is basically a question of keeping her in the best planing position. That means that the crew should keep the dinghy as upright as possible and should have their weight far enough aft to bring the bow clear of the water. There is no longer the danger of suction drag at the transom, for in properly designed boats in these conditions the water will flow

straight aft from the stern. The centre-board should be lowered at least a third to check sideslip and to give steerage control. The rudder should be in the vertical 90° position.

On hard runs the tuning of the rig is essentially a question of keeping the main-sail as smooth and flat as possible. Otherwise the dinghy will start that fearful rolling which occurs when the sail twists and the wind alternately streams past to windward and to leeward. The kicking-strap is therefore set up as tight as possible, and the mainsheet traveller is left to leeward. The foot is fairly taut, but the luff rather less so to ease the load on the mast. It is best to do without the jib in real planing conditions, but that is only possible in boats with a jib furler. Other-wise it is cleated as for moderate winds.

Correct technique in strong winds needs an acute feel for balance from the helms-man, for now it is a question of steering accurately to anticipate and counter the tendency to rolling. If the boat should, nevertheless, heel to windward the main-sail must be hardened in slightly to ensure that the wind blows on the windward side only and to increase the side force. Normally the main should be eased until it is just short of touching the lee shroud.

In hard weather too it is best if the helmsman sits to leeward and the crew to windward, but further aft in order to get the dinghy to plane better. In strong winds it is even more essential than in light or moderate winds to hoist the spin-naker to leeward of the jib and forestay, for this largely eliminates the danger of

General rule for spinnakers in hard winds: spinnakers kept close to the boat will fly more steadily but not pull so well. If the spinnaker is allowed to lift it will pull better but will not be so stable.

96

Here, in Force 5, the sails are setting well and pulling well, including the jib. The danger of capsizing is small with an experienced crew, so the spinnaker can be allowed to fly higher.

getting tangled up. Spinnaker hoisting is of course easier for those boats that have chutes. In very strong winds moving the weight aft naturally also increases stability because of the broader waterline aft. So, when setting the spinnaker, while the crew is busy hooking on the boom and downhaul, the lee sheet should be left free so that the spinnaker will not draw. Only when the crew has finished and moves aft should the spinnaker be allowed to fill by hauling in the sheet. It is advisable to check at a suitable moment that the spinnaker sheet has not caught itself up round the end of the boom when flapping around. The same holds good when lowering the spinnaker. The lee sheet is freed to empty the spinnaker of wind, again checking the end of the boom, and only then should the crew go forward, unhook the boom and downhaul and lower the sail, while the jib should already be drawing.

In strong winds the crew should not let the spinnaker ride so high, but should keep it closer to the boat, for it will then be more stable and not cause the boat to roll so much. Should the helmsman not be able to correct the tendency to roll by use of the mainsheet and by shifting weight, then the crew must help. To do this, when the boat heels to windward he should haul in on the spinnaker sheet, and when she heels to leeward he should pull back on the guy. This means that although the guy can be cleated it must be close to hand.

When sailing on the open sea, the dinghy cannot plane due to the height of the waves, but it will surf. The technique is basically the same as with a surf board.

Try to stay on the front of the advancing wave as long as possible. In this way the boat can sail faster than the wind which means that the boom will come in, particularly if there is a lull at that moment. In order to get the boat to surf, both crew pull in the spinnaker and mainsail sheets and, just for a second, move their weight forward at the very moment that the approaching wave lifts the stern. When the dinghy is surfing high on the face of the wave the crew shift their weight aft again, so that the bow cannot bore down into the trough of the wave. The helmsman tries to stay surfing as long as possible by luffing or bearing away slightly so as to maintain speed on the face of the wave.

When racing in strong winds such as this, there is always a gybe to be carried out, and this is without doubt the most difficult manoeuvre. Most capsizes occur at this time for it is not always clear when the conditions are most favourable for a gybe, nor what should be done. The easiest way usually is to gybe the boom over when there is a lull. In races, however, a boat must gybe on reaching the mark, and if the wind should ease at that moment it is pure luck.

As a basic rule then, gybe when the dinghy is sailing at maximum speed, but not when she is accelerating, for during acceleration the sails are under particularly heavy load which makes it very hard to bring the boom over. However, if the dinghy is sailing at maximum speed, the pressure on the sail is much less because of the smaller difference between the wind speed and the speed of the boat.

Worst of all, but only too often seen, is when an attempt is made to gybe when the dinghy has been stopped by a wave. The speed of the boat is then least, but it is only too easy to forget that the wind pressure on the sail is then at its maximum. This sort of thing must lead to a capsize, especially if the centreboard has not been raised at least half way. If this has been done it is possible that the dinghy may not 'trip over its own toes' and may perhaps bear away in time.

A typical capsize running after violent rolling. The sail is much too full making a large pocket and is eased too much whereby the wind alternately streams past to weather and to leeward thus causing rolling. Trim in the sail sharply to stop the roll.

Capsizing and Safety Precautions

Causes and Prevention of Capsizes

Looking at the various types of capsizes and the causes, it is plain that there are general distinct trends, and we will work on the basis that the spinnaker is set in winds up to Force 5. When running and beating capsizes occur most frequently to windward, but when reaching it is more usual for boats to capsize to leeward. The number of capsizes on the beat is less than those on reaches and runs. This can be explained by the simple fact that tacking is much less risky than gybing, and capsizes when manoeuvring account for a large proportion of the total. Purely on inland waters, such as alpine lakes with their gusty, fluky and often strong winds, there are frequent capsizes when beating, mostly to windward. The gusts here are not only difficult to see on the water, but often strike so sharply that even experienced helmsmen are not quick enough to bear away in time.

Most capsizes to leeward are caused by the following—listed in order of frequency:

With a spinnaker set on reaches: in a strong gust the dinghy becomes uncontrollable.

Unskilful gybing: the boat luffs up before the mainsheet is fully eased.

Pointing too high on a beat in hard gusts: this causes the dinghy to lose too much way and, with it, stability.

Likewise the main causes of capsizes to windward are:

Inability to steer a dinghy with spinnaker set when running.

Broad reaching: when rolling violently the hull slides away to leeward.

Too slow a reaction to a heading gust when beating.

If a sudden thunderstorm arrives, there are three ways to avoid a capsize: either lower all sail and rig a sea anchor, which is rarely carried; run dead before the wind under jib alone; or with an experienced crew, plane on a reach at full speed to the nearest shore. In this case it is essential that the dinghy should sail as fast as possible for the increased speed also increases the dynamic stability and thereby discourages a capsize. As soon as the dinghy comes off the plane she will capsize, and it makes no difference at all whether all the sails are fully eased or not—if it is a real thunderstorm. This third alternative is only effective on trapeze dinghies, for only then can the boat sail fast enough.

In doubtful weather conditions a possible capsize should be anticipated. That means tidiness on board, and life jackets, preferably with a collar, which must fit well without hindering freedom of movement. An anchor, a tow line and a bucket have given good service in many a critical situation. A line for righting the capsized boat has also proved useful, and the painter can be used for this. It must be attached where it can be reached easily, even if the boat has turned upside down, so could be attached to a fitting at the bow.

So as to react immediately and correctly in the event of a capsize it is as well to practise several times in bad weather. It will then be known roughly how the

101

boat will behave, and additionally the crew will to a certain extent be spared the physical shock which occurs on a first capsize. It is only those crews that take the right steps at the moment of capsizing who are able to reduce the consequences to a minimum.

What to do after a 180° Capsize

When the crew realise that a capsize is unavoidable efforts can immediately be concentrated on trying to prevent the boat turning turtle. This is not always possible when capsizing to windward for the crew will often be thrown right out of the boat. If someone finds himself under the mainsail he should make his way aft so as not to get caught up in the shrouds. It is pointless to come up under the sail to get air, for no air pockets can exist there.

Most light displacement dinghies have a tendency to turn upside down by virtue of their design. The side tanks often are

A classic capsize to leeward on a reach with the crew showing little sign of skill. The helmsman has not reacted quickly enough to a gust and has lost control of his Flying Dutchman. Using the tiller cannot help as the rudder blade is out of the water. Instead of letting the lee sheet fly the crew is trying hard to keep his weight to windward which is obviously accomplishing nothing.

too buoyant which causes the dinghy to ride very high in the water, and the resulting downward angle of the mast is therefore greater than with a boat which floats approximately half way, as is ideal. Actually turning right over is a safety factor, for if the crew have failed to maintain contact with the boat, its greater windage could otherwise cause it to drift away to leeward faster than a man could swim after it.

The best design, from this point of view, is undoubtedly a dinghy with narrow side decks and no side tanks. Instead a double bottom extends right to the sides with, of course, a partitioned off foredeck. The boat when capsized will then sink under

This could be the start of a classic capsize to windward. The boat was planing flat out when the gust eased suddenly. The trapeze hand is fully out on the wire. A little less wind now and a capsize to windward will be inevitable.

The upper picture shows the perfect floating position for a capsized boat where the tendency to turn right over is smallest.

103

water to about the fore-and-aft midships line, will not tend to turn turtle so easily, and will not drift away so fast if the crew is thrown out. Most moulded ply Flying Dutchmen are built in this way, but as this form of construction is more difficult and less strong in plastic, and there are further disadvantages such as the fact that the side decks are not so comfortable for the helmsman when sitting out, good designers often decide on a compromise by choosing narrow double-bottoms or half double-bottoms combined with relatively small side tanks.

When the dinghy has turned right over, the crew must fish around for the rope attached to the bow and lash it fast to the shroud attachment which is furthest downwind. If the centreboard has fallen right into the slot, which unfortunately is

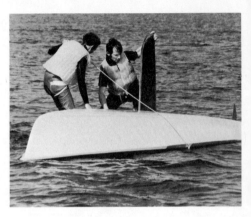

Most sailors behave as in this capsize to leeward. Even the best designed dinghies will turn turtle because of the crew's weight on the gunwale.

Second act. The dinghy has turned turtle and the crew have fished for a rope and fastened it to the shroud. This aid to righting is absolutely essential when the centreboard has slipped into the slot.

Situation No. 3 shows the two sailors as they are trying to pull the boat up with their feet on the lower gunwale and their bodies as far out as possible from the boat's hull.

The crew have got the boat into a horizontal position and provided there is nothing to be cleared (for example a spinnaker which should always be lowered) they can now bring her upright.

Success! The crew has got the boat upright. Watch out that the bow is pointing into the wind, or alternatively is at right angles to it with the crew to windward when she is righted.

Otherwise there is a danger that she will immediately capsize in the opposite direction.

The correct way to climb inboard. After the first man is in the boat and can balance her, the second man can clamber aboard. The sails are, of course, left absolutely free.

If the spinnaker is not lowered it makes it more difficult to right the boat because of the water that it carries. Should the boat nevertheless be righted it will often lead to a further capsize as the boat is so unstable.

105

usually the case, especially where the centreboard has been hoisted most of the way up on a run, this rope is the only way of getting the boat upright again. The rope is passed over the bottom so that the crew, bracing his feet on the gunwale, can heave on the rope with his body as far as possible away from the hull in order to get the greatest leverage. If the centreboard has not fallen into the slot it may not be necessary to use the rope, for the boat can then be righted by heaving strongly and rhythmically on the centreboard. Heaving on the mainsheet, as is often practised, does not really help, for that pulls the sail in tighter under water and this builds up increased resistance. It is a help to have a foam-filled mast, not because of the buoyancy aspect, but because no water can then find its way into the mast which would make righting the dinghy more difficult.

When the dinghy is floating horizontally, the centreboard must be set at its lowest position and the boat turned so that the mast is at right angles to leeward and the bow points directly towards the wind. Otherwise, on being righted, she will immediately capsize again in the opposite direction. If the spinnaker was set when she capsized it must now be stowed, for it is rarely possible to bring a dinghy upright with the spinnaker set. Main and jib sheets should be quite free so that the sails do not hold water and can flap

Rule No. 1 when capsizing. Immediately take all weight off the gunwale to discourage the tendency to turn turtle. Be careful with that centreboard: under such a load it could break.

freely when the boat is upright. The dinghy can now be righted by means of heaving on the centreboard and/or pulling on the rope. To ensure that she does not immediately capsize again when the first man climbs aboard the other member of the crew should swim forward and hold the bows into the wind. Once one person is safely aboard and can balance the boat, the second man can join him.

How to Avoid Turning Turtle

Eighty per cent of all capsizes need not lead to the boat turning bottom up if the crew know what to do. Misunderstandings between helmsman and crew are often the cause. Therefore when capsizing helmsman and crew should decide which of them can reach the centreboard quickest. The other could drop into the water to leeward and try to hold the mast up. The most important thing is to take all load off the gunwale as soon as possible, for that is the main cause of turning turtle. A dinghy hardly ever floats at right angles to the surface of the water, and the mast tends to tilt down into it. The weight of the crew on the gunwale increases this tendency so that turning turtle is the logical conclusion. So rule Number One when capsizing is: take the weight off the gunwale immediately.

Then, while one person immediately heaves and see-saws on the centreboard, the other can swim round to help him bring her horizontal. Having brought the bow head to wind he has two alternatives: either he can swim to the centreboard and help there, or he can go to the masthead, wait for a strong gust, and then shove the mast upwards hard so that the wind gets under the sail which helps the efforts of the man on the centreboard. This method is usual in single-handed dinghies like the Finn, and preferable because the centreboard method allows too much water to get into the boat. It is essential to keep hold of the painter when righting a boat by this method, because otherwise a single-hander will drift away out of reach after being righted. Which of these methods should be used in a two-man dinghy depends on the situation and circumstances. Usually both are effective, but if one method does not work, try out the other.

Immediate off-loading of the gunwale does not only discourage the boat from turning turtle but also means that dinghies with little side decking will have less water aboard after being righted and they will then be able to empty themselves when sailing. Frequently, however, there is so much water in the bottom that the dinghy has first to be baled out, for self-bailers are only effective when the dinghy is less than a third full of water. Otherwise the speed will be insufficient to allow the water to be sucked out of the bilges. A bucket, firmly attached, is never out of place and should always be carried in dinghies without double bottoms.

What to Do after Suffering Damage

Sometimes something breaks or gets lost in a capsize, and the dinghy has to be towed. Damage can also occur independently of capsizing, although the normal use of aluminium spars means that masts or booms seldom break. However, quite often the whole rig will collapse if a shroud, a stay or a fitting breaks. The rig, which will still be attached to the boat by means of all sorts of wires and ropes, should immediately be tidied up so that the hull is not damaged. The mast and other parts must be carefully lashed together before the tow-line is attached, and when under tow the centreboard should be hoisted two-thirds up. However, much damage is avoidable if the dinghy is carefully rigged before setting out, and if at the same time a careful check is made of all the parts and fittings that come under heavy load.

Righting a boat by pushing up the masthead mostly used in single-handed dinghies. The bow must be dead in the wind to allow the wind to get under the sail.

The photo overleaf shows what happens if the dinghy has insufficient fixed buoyancy. The crew has righted the boat but is not able to sail it empty.

109

An Introduction to Racing

The dinghy sailor is interested in sailing for sailing's sake—and really there is not much else that is possible because most dinghies are designed with that in mind, and not for use in any other way when actual sailing becomes of secondary importance. It is no wonder then that it is the dinghy sailor who first succumbs to the fascination of racing, particularly if he sails where there is little scope for cruising such as on inland waters which are often no larger than an old sandpit or reservoir. Can anything give more variety than racing? As it is on just such waters that an often astonishing amount of racing activity takes place, it is only a question of time before the racing bug strikes. The only ones that are safe from it are those who are dedicated to family sailing.

Prerequisites

The question should be answered before buying the boat as to whether the class on which one has set one's heart is raced in the area where one proposes to sail. Should it be too late, the boat already bought, and the fact established that there is no class-racing for the boat in the area, then everything is still not lost, for there is the possibility of racing against boats of different classes. All that is needed is to gather together at least a handful of keen boat owners who want to race and

As a beginner one should not start off in a giant field of top class sailors. The danger of collision or capsize is very great here, as one tricky situation follows another.

113

some people willing to act as race officers.

The best way of running such races is by using the Portsmouth Yardstick figures. These are handicap figures which have been established over the years by noting the average performance of different types of boats and comparing them with each other and with the basic boat. It is nevertheless best to take part in class racing, for handicap formulae such as the International Offshore Rules for ocean racers and, to a greater extent, the Portsmouth Yardstick tables are influenced by so many factors that they can never produce such fair results as class racing. Dinghy handicap racing should therefore never be taken in too deadly earnest.

When taking part in more or less improvised handicap races good boat handling and a basic knowledge of the racing rules are needed, but in class racing the rules should be thoroughly well known, and better handling is important. If a chance arises to crew several times for an experienced helmsman, grab it—for that is the best school there is.

Preparations for a Race

Before the first race there are, of course, a whole lot of things to check. To start with pay the entry fee and read the programme in good time. Beginners do well to put the race instructions, explanations and flag signals, together with a diagram of the course where necessary, in a transparent waterproof cover and stick them to the boat where they can easily be read. This avoids confusion over signals from the race officers. A race should be preceded by a good, nourishing but not too heavy meal, for both physical and nervous effort during a race use up calories just as much as loss of warmth in hard weather.

That the dinghy should be carefully rigged is obvious. The various shackles must be properly fastened, knots checked and bolts and pins which might work loose should be bound with sticky tape. In uncertain weather or strong winds, the crew should dress ready for racing before launching the boat, and not wait until they are sailing out to the start. Clothing should be warm, waterproof and should fit well without hindering movement. Safety jackets should be put on before setting out, or should at least be within easy reach in light airs. Until recently the choice of the right sail for the conditions was a major factor in deciding victory or defeat, but this does not have the same importance today due to the improvement in sail cloth, and even the leading crews now sail a whole season or longer with only one suit of sails.

On the way to the start the crew should concentrate on the boat, checking all the details again, and above all making sure that everything is stowed tidily in the right place, for when life becomes hectic or in the event of a capsize, disorder is the greatest enemy. If it is a run to the start which takes the boat through the area of the first beat, and races usually start with a beat, it is advisable to check on wind conditions so that they can be taken into account when deciding on tactics. A short warming-up before the start is also essential, and this should be undertaken gradually for muscles warm up slowly. An athlete, for example, will trot for half an hour to warm up before he makes the big effort. All manoeuvres should be practised to check that all equipment is functioning properly, and at the same time the dinghy can be properly trimmed. This is best done with the help of a friendly competitor in the same class whose speed is known, by sailing a trial run with the boats clear of each other's wind.

The Start

A good start is half the battle, so great care should be taken to get the best. First check that you understand the meaning of the flag and sound signals and that you know exactly where the starting line is. This is often an imaginary line between an inner mark in line with a mast or triangle on the starting vessel, and an outer mark at the other end of the line. Then wait with fingers poised to start the stopwatch as the gun goes ten minutes before the start or, better still, when a gun for a previous class goes. Alternatively a wrist-watch with a sweep second hand will do. Consider your tactics, bearing in mind that allowance must be made for changes in the wind during the last ten minutes. The first question is always: How, and at what part of the line shall I start? Decisive here is not only the direction of the wind, but also the position of the windward mark in relation to the starting line. The best place to start on the line will vary even when the relation between the direction of the wind and the position of the first mark alter only a little. There are innumerable variations but, in practice, unless the windward mark lies either to the extreme port or starboard of the starting line, it is the direction of the wind which determines the most favourable starting position. As a rule of thumb, start where the wind comes from. If it is blowing two or three degrees more from starboard, then the starboard side of the line must be the right place to start. If, on the contrary, the wind is coming slightly from port, then start to port. Strictly speaking the outside position is ideal in almost every case, whether at the port or starboard end of the line, for in only 5 per cent of races does the wind blow at exactly a right angle to the starting line. When this does happen either end will do in theory, although in practice there are other factors to take into account such as currents, tactical considerations for the first beat etc. which generally result in one side of the line being preferable to the other.

Normally then, the wind is not exactly at right angles to the line, so the problem is almost always whether to start at the point which happens to be the most advantageous at that moment, or whether to concentrate on starting at that point which will be best for the first beat. It can happen that the optimum starting position and the best place for starting the beat coincide, and then the decision is clear. If they do not, then the choice should fall on the best position for the first beat. After the start get on to the better tack as soon as you can.

At the five minute gun any necessary correction can be made to the watch. With this gun, course signals will appear if they have not already been given, and racing rules come into force. It is now important to concentrate entirely on reaching the selected starting position at the right moment, and the lighter the wind the earlier one should do this, for

G 1679 has got a classic leeward start. He has crossed the line at full speed, has no-one to leeward and is in the safe leeward position by comparison with his competitors to windward.

116

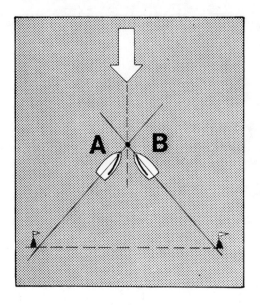

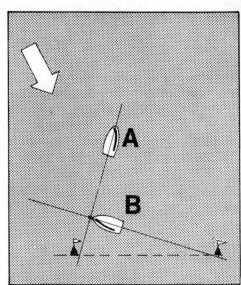

frequently the wind will ease in the five minute period and make it impossible to reach the best place. Naturally, if the wind shifts the best place will also change before the start, so it is wise not to be inflexibly determined on one particular spot.

And now to the start itself. The most important rule is: cross the line at full speed as the gun goes, and sail on as freely and with as clear a wind as possible. To get full way on, it is necessary to bear away a few seconds before the start. Shortly before the gun goes, therefore, you should be considerably to windward of any boats that may be to leeward. This safety gap is particularly important because it is the only guarantee of being able to sail at full speed after the start, without being forced to pinch to get clear of the backwind from leeward boats. It is best

to have room to windward too for then, after a perhaps unfortunate start, the boat will not have to lie hopelessly sandwiched between other boats, but can go about and try to beat clear. If your boat is one of the few with a clear wind fairly soon after the start, then you are holding all the trumps.

The Race Course

After the start the same holds good: sail the course as clear of, and unhindered by competitors as you feel is right. The need for clear wind need not be carried to such an extreme as to cause you to make tacks far from the other boats unless this is because you are so far in the lead! It is only advisable to take an extreme course if you are hopelessly at the tail end of the fleet, when taking a long shot could not make matters worse. Otherwise tack

If the wind on this diagram is blowing at right angles to the starting line it does not matter where on the line one starts. A starting position should then be chosen which will give the best direction for the ensuing beat.

If there are no other considerations to take into account, start from the side from which the wind is blowing. A is already far ahead of B a few minutes after the start.

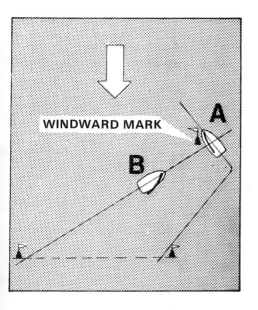

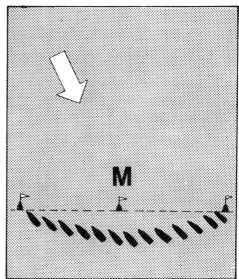

On the next drawing the windward buoy was not at right angles to the middle of the line. B has to reach down to the mark with eased sheets. A has a shorter distance to sail and therefore gets there first.

The last drawing shows how most of the middle boats lie further behind the line if the outer marks are a long way apart. A middle buoy (M) is then a great help to starting. Below, the start of a giant fleet.

119

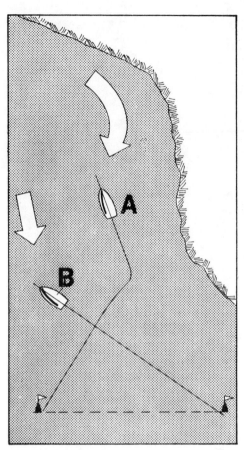

Here A has used the wind sensibly and is sailing in a favourable slant by the shore. After tacking A is far ahead of B.

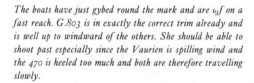

The boats have just gybed round the mark and are off on a fast reach. G.803 is in exactly the correct trim already and is well up to windward of the others. She should be able to shoot past especially since the Vaurien is spilling wind and the 470 is heeled too much and both are therefore travelling slowly.

so that you are sailing where the best conditions are to be expected, and watch out that you lose as little ground as possible in the event of an unfavourable wind shift. There is little point in indulging in battles with individual boats while the rest of the fleet sails on out of sight. A good sailor can be spotted quickly because he continuously reviews the situation as a whole. Sailing the optimum course and at the same time covering other competitors almost always means compromise.

The types of race course usual today are, first the Olympic course which consists of three marks laid shortly before the start so that they can be sited by the race officers in their correct positions for the wind of the moment. The Olympic course is usually left-about, and consists of two triangular rounds with one straight up and down. Another type of course consists of a number of buoys in a circle with a starting line in the middle. The race officers can then lay a starting line at right angles to the wind wherever it comes from. A full length course consists of two triangular rounds and one straight up and down, and might be sailed left or right-about. Then there are special courses which are set when triangular courses with equal length legs cannot be laid due to the shape of the water. For example it is quite impossible to set a circle of buoys on some of the alpine lakes which are narrow or small reservoirs. These courses, too, attempt to give a fair proportion of beating, running and reaching.

The lower picture shows an ideal defensive position. G.1527 lies clear ahead and from here can cover all attacks by G.1216.

How can I get fit?

The dinghy sailor cannot benefit from his technical knowledge if he is unable to put it into use because he is not physically fit, and fitness unfortunately is only too often underrated. Obviously in winds of over Force 3 a dinghy crew will not be able to get a boat to sail at its fastest unless they are in good physical condition. If they are not, their ability to react quickly and to concentrate will be reduced. Nor will they be able to sit the dinghy out properly.

A sensible training programme specifically suited to the dinghy sailor is an unavoidable essential for people who take their sailing seriously, unless they are already doing enough in other ways to be in good shape.

By comparison with other sportsmen a dinghy sailor is subject to quite different stresses, so it will be useful to underline the main points. In light airs he must be supple and able to move smoothly and cat-like so as not to upset the forward motion of the boat. In this weather he also needs to be able to stay still for long periods in one position without loss of concentration. In stronger winds he needs to be able to sit out or stand out and must have great stamina. When manoeuvring he must move quickly and surely.

So he must be able to use his strength over long periods and must develop speed of movement. He must also be able to control his strength accurately and both helmsman and crew, but especially the trapeze hand, must have particularly good balance. Typical sailing conditions require the helmsman to sit out, and the crew too if the boat has no trapeze, while the trapeze position for the crew calls for strength in the legs, the stomach muscles, the arms and the back.

The trapeze stance and sitting out are the normal state of affairs for dinghy sailors and puts them under a lot of strain.

125

There are training programmes which can be undertaken under a qualified trainer, and the all round training designed for a skier is always of benefit. But a sailor can work out his own training programme at home, and should not only train before fitting out his boat but in the summer too, when he can improve his fitness, even if with a reduced programme.

It is best to train two to four times weekly, or daily for a shorter period with a longer session once or twice a week. A session should last from 15–60 minutes in front of an open window so as to absorb sufficient oxygen into the lungs. Start with warming up exercises to stretch the ligaments and tendons and to warm the muscles. For details of a training programme please turn to page 128.

Modern dinghy sailing has recently become a truly high performance sport, and the man who does not have the necessary physical fitness will not be able to handle his boat properly.

126

EXERCISES

Warming up exercises (5–10 minutes)

With legs straight and astride and feet flat on the floor:
> Make vertical circles with straight arms first forwards and then backwards.
> Move the hips in as large a circle as possible.
> Swing the pelvis from side to side and bend sideways from the waist in the opposite direction, hands on hips.
> With the hips stationary swing the upper part of the body in a circle, hands on hips.
> Move the elbows in as large a circle as possible.

Gentle hopping on the spot.
Gentle trotting on the spot.
Arms upward stretch.
Touch toes with straight legs.

Specific training (15–50 minutes)

1st Exercise:
5–15 high jumps standing on the spot.
5–15 jacknifes, touch toes and straighten.
5–15 press-ups, keep body straight.

2nd Exercise:
1–5 minutes stand back to the wall at 45° with shoulders resting on wall.
10–30 times bicycle the legs in the air, lying on your back.
5–15 press-ups, keep body straight.

3rd Exercise:
15–40 knee bends.
5–10 times bend the hips (sitting on a stool with feet under a cupboard or chest, hands behind the head, lean back).
3–10 pull-ups under the edge of a table or on a ladder. Keep body straight.

4th Exercise:
10–20 times hip rolls. Lie on your back, legs straight in the air, slowly lower to the side.
5–10 times change weight from one foot to the other in a crouching position.
5–10 times raise legs high straight when lying on the floor on your back.

5th Exercise:
3–5 times lift arms and knees from the floor while lying on the stomach.
10–30 times step onto a chair and down again.
3–10 pull-ups under the table edge.

Pause from 15–30 seconds after each exercise and repeat them as often as you wish. Concentrate on those exercises which strengthen the weakest points. If the arms are not strong enough increase the arm exercises. It is important to practise all the exercises rapidly and exactly for only then will they fulfil the aim.